It Works for Me!

Shared Tips for Teaching

Hal Blythe
Foundation Professor of English
Eastern Kentucky University

Charlie Sweet
Foundation Professor of English
Eastern Kentucky University

NEW FORUMS PRESS INC.
Stillwater, Oklahoma, U.S.A.

International Standard Book Number: 0-913507-95-4

TABLE OF CONTENTS

ACKNOWLEDGEMENTS

We would like to thank our typist, Anne Norton, for all her help with this book.

Hal Blythe
Charles Sweet

NOTE

The following works have previously appeared in publications:

The Thirty Second Stratagem: An Opening Gambit. Originally published in *The Teaching Professor* (May, 1997), by Magna Publications, Inc., Madison, WI.

The Time Capsule: An Excercise. Originally published in *The Teaching Professor* (November, 1997) by Magna Publications, Inc.m Madison, WI.

It Works For Me

INTRODUCTION

L ast week one of our long-time colleagues remarked on the difference between her class presentations today and those of her early years. Sure, Marsha admitted, now she's more at home with the material and more certain of herself as a teacher. But those weren't the only reasons for the differences.

Back then, Marsha claimed, she had based her teaching almost entirely on theory; she had listened dutifully to the director of the program, who loaded her down with statistics and charts designed to reveal what *ought* to go on in the typical classroom. It didn't take our colleague long to realize that the ideal and the real classroom are farther apart than Mars and Venus: many of those theoretical approaches simply didn't work in the "field."

Like Marsha, all of us want to be effective teachers. Since our earliest days in the classroom, we have read books and articles about pedagogy, attended relevant conferences and workshops, and talked with colleagues as well as students—all with the purpose of improving our performance for those few minutes each day that help define our degree of success in our profession.

No matter how thoroughly we prepare or how hard we execute, though, some presentations just seem to work while others fall flat. Some days we stride from the classroom buoyed by the knowledge that the day's material really got through to students. Other times we drag ourselves out the door feeling the previous hour an almost total waste.

Is there a handy-dandy, sure-fire, one-size-fits-all method to insure success in the classroom? Of course not. So many variables exist within each class we teach: subject matter, number of students, nature of students (e.g. major, age, experience, desire, learning style, G.P.A.), time of class, classroom arrangement. Each class experience presents its own problems and potentials. Even we as teachers come to each class with different degrees of knowledge, interest, and motivation, and obviously we're a bit more enthusiastic about the new class we created than that Freshman section we're teaching for the tenth straight semester.

So why bother to read yet another book about teaching? What can you possibly gain that will prepare you to meet those daily moments of truth?

Perhaps this book's title suggests the answer. *It Works for Me: Shared Tips for Teaching* is not a treatise on pedagogical theory, nor is it designed to dictate a set of rules for success in the classroom. Its purpose is not to provide you with a complete program for better teaching. *It Works for Me* is simply a collection of practical tips drawn from the real-life experiences of some of Kentucky's outstanding college teachers across the disciplines. It is meant as an aid for any instructor who feels the need for a little something extra from time to time to raise the classroom experience from merely passable to one from which students will eagerly learn and one they will remember.

Use *It Works for Me* as a ready reference tool, pulling from it tips, techniques, and assignments and tailoring them to fit your unique style and situation. If a technique works, continue to employ it, shaping and expanding it so that it becomes your own. If something doesn't quite suit your needs, modify it or toss it out. Perhaps some of the suggestions will even whet your appetite, leading to the creation of new, exciting materials of your own.

We have acceded to individual colleague's wishes. Occasionally you will run across uncredited entries because the tipsters preferred to remain anonymous.

It Works for Me will not necessarily make you an effective teacher. What it will do is supply you with useful techniques to get the most from your classroom experience.

I. THE FIRST DAY

Perhaps no class meeting is more important than the first. While some teachers use the time for a hurried introduction, a few handouts and an assignment, experienced instructors realize that much more is at stake than a mere beginning to the semester.

Effective teachers use that first period not only to introduce themselves and the course, but also to establish clear objectives/goals for the semester and establish an atmosphere conducive to learning. In addition, the first meeting allows the instructor to get to know a little about the students (background, interests, expectations) as well as encouraging them to meet each other and strike up relationships that will benefit them as individuals and the class as a whole.

An effective first meeting doesn't come by accident. You have so few minutes to accomplish so many things without making your students think they've entered the world of fast-forward teaching.

Planning is essential, and here are a few tips from teachers who get the most from their initial meeting.

Icebreakers

The 3x5 Card

On the first day of class, I give each of my students a 3x5 card on which he/she provides information about him/herself that makes my getting to know the class a lot easier. In addition to material on my students' background, the card provides me with important information in case of an emergency during the semester.

General Information for the 3x5 card:

- Name: Last Name, first name (nickname)
- Social Security Number
- Current address and phone
- Permanent address and phone
- Class (i.e., Freshman, Sophomore, etc.)
- Major - Advisor
- Previous Math - where applicable
- Name and address (city and state) of high school
- What other courses are you taking in our department this semester
- Hobbies

Amy King
Eastern Kentucky University

The 3x5 Card +

On the first day of class, I have each student fill out a 3x5 index card with name, address, phone number, SS#, and major. Then, they are to turn the card over and tell me something interesting about themselves. This can be anything from the number of children they have to their life's goal. I make it a point to learn the students' names very early by using a seating chart, and having these little tidbits really helps me to associate the name with the face.

Laura Denton
Maysville Community College

The Student Questionnaire

I use a student questionnaire on the first day of every class. It asks the student for basic information along with a few "break the ice" questions like: what adjective best describes you? On the back of the response form I ask the students to introduce themselves to me in a paragraph or two and perhaps to comment on something that we will cover in class early in the semester. I find this is an effective and efficient way to use the first 20 minutes or so of the first class meeting to learn as much about my students as possible and to indicate to them in a nonthreatening way that I am interested in them as individuals. This activity is followed by my telling them about myself in "a paragraph or two" before going on with the essential details of the course. If time allows, this activity can also be followed by small group discussions in which 5-6 students use the questionnaires to get acquainted with other members of the group.

POL 101/ Student Questionnaire

GENERAL INFORMATION FOR THE STUDENT QUESTION-NAIRE:

Name
Mailing Address (Local and/or Campus)
Local Phone
If you work, please describe your job and its time commitments
Major
Hometown

Concerns:

• What concerns or worries, if any, do you have about this course?

• Professionally speaking, what would you like to be doing ten years from now?

- What do you consider to be your greatest strength? Your greatest weakness?
- What adjective best describes you?
- If you voted in the last presidential election, for whom did you vote?
- Why (briefly)?
-

On the back of this sheet, please write:

- A paragraph or two introducing yourself to me. Tell me a little bit about your family, school background, hobbies, or other important matters you would be wiling to share.
- A one or two sentence definition of the word "politics." One or two sentences about your earliest memory of something "political" that you experienced or observed.

Paul Blanchard
Eastern Kentucky University

The Self-Introduction

In the first or second class session, have the students introduce themselves and tell where they are from, regardless of the number of students in the class or the nature of the class. Pay close attention to them to let them know that you care about them. You can also make note of where each student is from or observe something about each student. This information helps you remember names by association. Doing this seems to make a tremendous difference in "setting the stage" for a good class.

Steve Fardo
Eastern Kentucky University

The Roster

In the first week or so of classes, I pass around a sheet of paper for the students to write their name and home phone number, make copies and give one to each student. This way, if the students must be absent, they can call someone to get notes or find out if there is an assignment due for the next class, or discuss homework problems. Sometimes, students who have been in a class of mine before will ask for the list at the first class meeting. The list also helps students to become better acquainted and, therefore, be more friendly in the classroom.

Laura Denton
Maysville Community College

The Collage

This is an introductory exercise that I find works well in a variety of classes and with students at all levels. I have each student make a collage to share with the class. I briefly explain what a collage is, and I tell the students that their collage should be about themselves and somehow represent the different roles that they play in their lives. We briefly discuss what some of those roles might be—student, parent, sibling, employee, child, etc. How each student makes his or her collage is entirely up to that student.

I have students make their collages during class, and on that day I bring to class magazines, glue sticks, paste, color markers, etc., which I have students share, and enough large sheets of colored paper so that each student can choose a piece to use as a background for the collage. I don't bring scissors because I find that students are freer to create when they have to tear the pictures and works instead of cutting them.

After students are finished making their collage (about $\frac{1}{2}$ hour), in a small class I have students take turns introducing themselves to the class, showing their collages, and explaining what the various images represent. With a large class, I break the students into groups of 4-5 students and have the students show their collage and explain to their group.

In writing classes, I have students explain their collage in writing. Besides explaining the images, I ask students to consider the significance of their choice of background color, the placement of the images on the page, the grouping of images, etc. In my developmental classes, this writing evolves into a short essay.

I find students generally realize that their audience will not understand what the various pieces of the collage mean without some interpretation. Also, students generally have a lot to say about their collage, which helps facilitate an early writing assignment.

In both literature and writing classes, I use this recent creative experience to start a discussion of the creative process—how it is different for different people, how it always involves choices, etc.

I find that students start talking among themselves as they share the materials for the collage. This "breaks the ice" and gets students to begin relating to each other. Sharing and explaining their collage is an easy way for students to introduce themselves to me and their classmates. Instead of the "where I went to high school and what I'm majoring in" variety of introductions that I get if I leave students to their own devices, I find most students willing to share less generic information about themselves as they explain the various parts of their collage. These introductions help me too as I'm trying to put a name with a face early in the semester. Also, I think this initial sharing is an important first step to successful collaborative learning, which I encourage through the use of group work throughout the semester.

Sandy Eubanks
Jefferson Community College

Getting Acquainted

In order to enliven a class, build interest, or illustrate a point experientially, I like to use "icebreakers" that help students get better acquainted by having them mix and interview each other until they identify persons with predetermined characteristics related to course content. For instance, in a geography class, students can be asked to identify someone for each of the following categories: Lived on a farm, in a city, on an island, or in another country. In addition to getting acquainted, in a well designed icebreaker students become aware of the diverse experiences available as a class resource.

William Jones
Eastern Kentucky University

Picture Books

Each semester I photograph students (3/shot), develop the pictures, and photocopy the pictures with the students identified for my class. It helps the class in a number of ways, including helping me learn all their names, and helps them know each other's name. With the new digital cameras available this will be even easier!

Kathy Mowers
Owensboro Community College

How to Use a Textbook (Correctly)

I am a firm believer in the use of a textbook as a pedagogical tool in the learning process. I have found that, unfortunately, my students do not know how to correctly use a college textbook. They think that if they just read a chapter, that's all they need do. As a result, I spend a few minutes at the beginning of each of my courses with the following brief discourse.

> Books are the carriers of civilization. Without books, history is silent, literature dumb, science crippled, thought and speculation at a standstill. They are engines of change, windows on the work, lighthouses erected in a sea of time.
> — Barbara Tuchmann

Your textbook is one the most important learning tools in any course and should be very carefully and conscientiously used. I have found the following approach to using a textbook to be very effective.

1. **Survey**. Briefly scan the chapter to become familiar with its general content. Quickly read the title and major headings. If there is a list of chapter concepts and a chapter outline, pay close attention to these. This survey will give you a feel for the topic and how the chapter is approaching it.

2. **Question**. As you scan each section, compose one important question that this section will answer. This question will help focus your later reading of the section.

3. **Read**. Carefully read each section. Read to understand concepts and major points, and try to find the answer to your question (see point number 2). You

---

may want to highlight very important terms or concepts, but do not fall into the trap of indiscriminantly highlighting everything. Pay attention to any terms printed in boldface or color since the author(s) usually consider these to be very important.

4. **Revise**. After reading each section, revise your initial question to more accurately reflect the section's contents. These questions can be written in the margin of your text in pencil.

5. **Record.** Underline or highlight with a different color (see number 3) those sentences that answer the question. You may wish to write down the answer in note form as well. This process will give you good material to use in preparing for exams.

6. **Review**. Review the information by trying to answer your questions for each section without looking at the book. If your book has a list of key words or a set of study questions, be sure to use these in your review. You will retain much more if you review the material several times.

John Harley
Eastern Kentucky University

Empathy

Try to put yourself mentally in the place of your students. Do all you can to cause students to enjoy your class. Use a variety of techniques—lecture, discussion, demonstration, questioning, application activities, review, humor—to encourage interactive learning. Be aware of methods which seem to work best for you. We should capitalize on our strengths and try to minimize our weaknesses as teachers.

Steve Fardo
Eastern Kentucky University

Names and Faces

On the first day of class, I often give students a little written exercise. I ask them to write their names in the upper right hand corner of the first page before they begin. As they write, I walk among them and memorize all their names and faces. Then, at the end of the period, or at the second class meeting, I look at them and call on them **by name**. I never explain how I do it...but they always seem to appreciate being "somebody." It certainly makes them more willing participants in class discussion.

> Ron Wolfe
> Eastern Kentucky University

Reading Survey

Over the years I've stopped assuming students can/like to read. Therefore, one of the many things I hand out the first day is this reading survey. On one hand, the results give me information on each individual, and on the other the results help me gauge the class' general reading background, including their attitudes toward the printed word. Another benefit of the survey is that it subtly underscores to the student the importance of reading—both in my course and in their lives. I've found this instrument more effective than simply announcing to the students something so platitudinous as "reading is important" or "Read as if your life depended upon it."

Survey

DIRECTIONS: Circle your response:
1. How many newspapers do you read on an average day?
   - a. 0
   - b. 1
   - c. 2
   - d. 3 or more
2. How many magazines do you read in an average week?
   - a. 0
   - b. 1
   - c. 2
   - d. 3 or more
3. How many non-school-related books (fiction or non-fiction) did you read in the past year?
   - a. 0
   - b. 1
   - c. 2
   - d. 3 or more

4. Did the home you grew up in contain newspapers?
   a. yes   b. no
5. Did the home you grew up in contain magazines?
   a. yes   b. no
6. Did the home you grew up in contain books?
   a. yes   b. no
7. Do you recall seeing your parent(s) reading?
   a. yes   b. no
8. Did your parent(s) read to you as a child?
   a. yes   b. no
9. What did you spend the most time in your youth doing?
   a. watching TV   b. reading
10. With today's electronic technology—such as computers, video- and audiotapes, electronic teleconferencing, and satellite communication—reading is of little importance.
    a. I agree   b. I disagree
11. When I read something, such as a course assignment, I must read every word.
    a. I agree   b. I disagree
12. It is extremely difficult to improve reading skills; if I am an average or below-average reader, I will probably stay that way.
    a. I agree   b. I disagree
13. Everything that is read should be read the same way.
    a. I agree   b. I disagree
14. Circle any of the following you do when reading textbooks.
    a. underline/highlight key terms
    b. make marginal notations
    c. write marginal questions/comments
    d. take notes
    e. keep the book pure for better resale value

Charlie Sweet
Eastern Kentucky University

The Characteristics of Literature

In any introductory lit course, on the first day I hand out this list. It reflects the basic knowledge that I think (I used to assume) every student taking the course ought to have at that point. Not only does it codify what is expected, but it gets the student up to speed immediately. In addition, it acclimates the student to the "naming of names." The Chinese have an old saying: "The beginning of wisdom is learning to call things by their right name." The beginning of success in any class is learning the nomenclature of the field, which in my case is learning to call the elements of literature by their right name ("No, Virginia, each piece of literature is *not* a story").

So, from Day II on when I discuss how a story is told, I expect each student to grasp the name "method of narration." Obviously one of the students' first homework assignments is to learn the handout.

Students like the list because it lets them know from the first day exactly what they're expected to know.

The Characteristics of Literature

I. **Genres** (not all literature is a "story")
   A. Poem: indicated by " " (e.g. "Rape of the Lock")
   B. Drama / Play: indicated by _____ (e.g. *Phaedra*)
   C. Short Story: indicated by " " (e.g. "Ligeia")
   D. Novel: indicated by _____ (e.g. *Madame Bovary*)

II. **Basic Elements**
   A. Character: the who, the protagonist
   B. Plot: the sequence of what happens
   C. Setting: where and when the work takes place
   D. Point of View / Method of Narration: how the story is told

III. **Expectations** (what you should know about the assignment before class)
   A. characters: who are the major ones
   B. what happens / surface action
   C. dialogue (major points of what is said)
   D. where the work takes place (location, time frame, era)
   E. narrator (whose point of view is used—e.g. a character?)

IV. **Things to Consider About your Reading**
   A. The work's relationship to its age (beliefs, events, philosophies)
   B. Theme: what overall points does the work make?
   C. Its relationship to other works (both contemporary and from other eras)
   D. Your evaluation of the work (e.g. does it get across a point to you?)

Charlie Sweet
Eastern Kentucky University

How To Answer an Essay Question

With the renewed interest in writing in all disciplines, more and more instructors are using the essay question. To help my students get through the sometimes formidable task of composing an essay, I've compiled a list of helpful hints. I usually hand it out the period before an essay test as I consider it part of my review (in nearly all my classes, I spend the period before a test reviewing format, past tests, points of emphasis, etc.). While my students are taking the actual essay test, I allow them to keep this handout beside them as a constant guide.

For courses in which lots of writing is required, I give students the "tip sheet" the first day of class.

How to Answer an Essay Question

I. **Avoid these Pitfalls**:
   1. Cliches
   2. Jargon
   3. Stilted Language
   4. Failure to be Selective and Specific
   5. Glittering Generalities
   6. Memory, not Mastery
   7. Superlatives Instead of Insightful Comments
   8. Failure to Read the Question Carefully
   9. No Thesis
   10. Lack of Mechanics

II. **Remember these Rules:**

1. Language must clarify rather than cloud meaning.
2. Always deliberately and specifically confront the question.
3. Be selective in using materials.
4. Always organize around a thesis.

III. **Follow these Six Steps**:

1. Read and thoroughly understand the question.
2. Jot down random, relevant thoughts.
3. Derive a comprehensive statement (your Thesis) from these notes that answers the question.
4. Structure the essay to support the thesis.
5. Construct support paragraphs using the reasons listed in the outline/thesis statement.
6. Proofread.

Hal Blythe
Eastern Kentucky University

The Reasoning Process

A common student complaint is, "I know what I want to say, but I don't know how to say it." One solution for turning thoughts into print is a one-page format I give my students. The format contains a step-by-step process moving from the theoretical to the very practical. I have even included a checklist to make certain students follow the format.

The format has several advantages:

- Variety. It can be used for almost any paper (or speech) in almost any discipline.
- Ease in following.
- Simplicity. It takes students from the broadest level of generality down to specific detail.
- Compactness. It's theoretical and practical.

The Reasoning Process
The Situation: you have a viewpoint/an opinion (an attitude you hold concerning a particular subject).

The Purpose: you ask yourself why you feel the way you do.

The Theoretical Procedure:
1. Identify the limits and the scope of your subject.
2. Establish exactly what you feel about this subject—i.e. your opinion.
3. Explain why you think your viewpoint is valid—i.e. the reasons for your opinion.
4. Elaborate why you think each reason is valid—i.e. your proof.

The Practical Approach:
1. Brainstorm. Jot down on a piece of paper any reason or piece of proof for your opinion.
2. Do not bother initially with separating reasons and pieces of proof.
3. Do not bother initially with making well-thought-out statements.
4. Sort your information into groups by placing the relevant proof with the appropriate reason.
5. Develop additional information for incomplete areas.

The Checklist (from thought to writing; from you to your reader):
1. Introductory Unit
_____ a. Did you catch your reader's interest?
_____ b. Did you introduce your subject?
_____ c. Did you limit your subject's scope?
_____ d. Did you clearly state your opinion?
_____ e. Did you list the reasons for your opinion?

2. Development Unit (repeated three times)
_____ a. Did you provide a transition?
_____ b. Did you restate your opinion?
_____ c. Did you restate the one reason your paragraph will treat?
_____ d. Did you define or amplify your reason if needed?
_____ e. Did you provide two major supports for your reason?
_____ f. Did you provide two pieces of proof for each major support?
_____ g. Did you pull the paragraph together with a tie-up?
3. Concluding Unit
_____ a. Did you provide a transition?

_____ b. Did you restate your opinion?
_____ c. Did you restate your reasons for the opinion?
_____ d. Did you disengage yourself?

Hal Blythe
Eastern Kentucky University

Common Spelling Problems

The comment used to be, "I don't have to know how to spell. When I get out of school, I'll have a secretary to do that." Now the reasoning is, "Don't computers have Spellcheck?"

The truth is that even the semi-miraculous Spellcheck can't find homophones and has trouble with other forms. To help my orthographically challenged students, I've prepared this short list of the most common spelling errors (to be used only in desperate circumstances, of course).

Common Spelling Problems

I. Confusion With Homophones/Sound-Alikes

accept - except	principal - principle
affect - effect	quiet - quite
allude - elude	stationary - stationery
complement - compliment	than - then
dyeing - dying	their - there - they're
elicit - illicit	to - too - two
eminent - imminent	weather - whether
loose - lose	were - where
moral - morale	your - you're

II. Failure To Use Proper Past Tense (terminal -ed)
ask - asked
use - used

III. Fused Words

alot (a lot)	eventhough (even though)
alright (all right)	noone (no one)

IV. Misspelled Words

analyze	persuade
athlete	receive
definite	similar
embarrass	succeed
environment	tries
existence	truly
leisure	villain
necessary	writing
neither	

V. Wrong Usage

already - all ready	awhile - a while
altogether - all together	everyone - every one
anyone - any one	someone - some one

Anon.

Ten Timely Tips

Sometimes I think that it's just my students who have trouble making the subject and verb of a sentence agree or learning not to dangle a modifier. Then I get a call from across campus with a colleague wondering whether it's "who" or "whom" or if it's O.K. to split an infinitive.

While no one can hope to know all the rules in the grammar handbook, we all need to be confident to share a few basic tips with our students. So here's a list of what I've found are the most common questions (and, no, I don't care if you split an infinitive).

Ten Timely Tips on Grammar

1. A *PHRASE* is a group of related words without a subject and a predicate.
2. A *SUBORDINATE / DEPENDENT CLAUSE* is a group of words containing both a subject and predicate that is still not a sentence.
3. A MAIN / INDEPENDENT CLAUSE (usually called a complete sentence) is neither a phrase nor a dependent clause. A phrase or dependent clause can be a part of a sentence, but not a complete

sentence. To determine this distinction, apply the TWO **TESTS FOR SENTENCE COMPLETENESS**:

> a. Does the word group have both a subject and a predicate? (If so, it cannot be a phrase)
>
> b. Does the word group have a subordinator? (If not, it cannot be a dependent clause)

4. Four types of sentences exist:

> a. Simple (one subject + one predicate)
>
> b. Compound (minimum of two main clauses)
>
> c. Complex (minimum of one main clause + one subordinate clause)
>
> d. Compound-Complex (minimum of two main clauses + one subordinate clause)

5. Five ways exist to link independent / main clauses (MC):

> a. MC. MC.
>
> b. MC, (coordinating conjunction) MC.
>
> c. MC; MC.
>
> d. MC: MC.
>
> e. MC—MC.

6. Main clauses **cannot** be linked by:

> a. a comma with no FABONSY (for, and, but, or, not, so, yet) conjunction (MC, MC. = comma splice)
>
> b. no punctuation (MC MC. = fused/run-on sentence).

7. A modifier should be placed as close as possible to the element it modifies to avoid **misplaced modification**.

8. A modifier must clearly and logically modify another element to avoid **dangling modification**.

9. A predicate **must agree in number** with its subject.

10. A pronoun **must agree in number** with its antecedent (the word to which the pronoun refers).

Ten More Tips

1. Do not use **this** by itself (always follow **this** with a noun).
2. Do not use **you** to refer either to yourself or all people.
3. Do not substitute **would be** for the present or past tense.
4. Avoid redundancies such as **the reason why** or **is because**.
5. Avoid **when** and **where** after **is** in definitions.

6. Do not use **that** to refer to a person.

7. Avoid opening sentences with **There is, There are**, and **It is** when possible.

8. Do not open a sentence with **An example**.

9. Avoid double punctuation marks such as **!!** or **??.**

10. Follow an introductory subordinate clause with a comma.

Hal Blythe
Eastern Kentucky University

The ARTS System of Success

On the first day of class, after I'd given out the zillionth handout and said what I thought was the final word of introduction, I always asked if anyone had a question. Invariably, one of the pragmatic generation responded with something like, "Dr. Sweet, what's it gonna take for me to get a good grade in here?" As a result, I've evolved still one more handout.

The ARTS System is an acronym that condenses what I consider the four major steps to success in my class. The ARTS acronym has the advantages of being easy to remember and suggestive of my subject area, but I stress that it can be used to help the student succeed in all disciplines.

Hints for Success

Attend class regularly so that you can fully participate.

Read the material completely and on time.

Take comprehensive and systematic notes. Don't depend on just your memory. If you miss class, get the notes from another student.

Study your notes. Take a few minutes every day to read over that day's notes. Jot down questions to ask in class.

Charlie Sweet
Eastern Kentucky University

II. GETTING STARTED

Just as the first class meeting sets the stage and establishes the atmosphere for the entire semester, so the first few minutes of each session can dictate its success or failure. Too often teachers are content to trudge into class, plop down their books, and mechanically call the roll. Their students—who have raced from other classes, dragged themselves from dorm beds, or fought traffic to find a parking space—are encouraged to slump into their seats and think about that pick-up ballgame after lunch or their hot date the night before.

Rather than promoting boredom, these initial moments can be used positively to signal the beginning of class, draw students into the material, and provide direction for the remainder of the session. If the first minutes accomplish these goals, you have the chance of a great class. Without these moments being positive...

Following are some ways you can use those first minutes of class to increase your odds for a successful hour.

The Thirty-Second Strategem

Television calls the technique "The Teaser." So as ER begins on Thursday night, its audience is greeted by a near-blink-of-the-eye scene. Eager to learn what new relationship or life-saving opportunity will fall into the laps of Dr. Doug or Nurse Hathaway, viewers refuse to budge, or even worse, channel surf.

While college instructors are rarely recruited from the ranks of network television or Las Vegas lounge acts, I've found that all of us can learn something from the world of entertainment. Too often teachers begin their classes with techniques that inadvertently turn off rather than turn on their students. Ask yourself, how many times have you begun the period by mechanically calling the roll, making departmental announcements, giving next Tuesday's assignment, or reminding the class of the Big Test next week?

No study would refute that teaching works best in an interactive format—a cool medium as Marshall McLuhan put it. Engaging your vidkid students' minds immediately is important. And you want them to be active thinkers, not merely passive recorders. The opening moments, then, can be the most important in making or breaking a class. Let me suggest what I call the Thirty-Second Strategem, a technique that if properly employed breaks down the student-teacher barrier, fosters a positive atmosphere of learning, and draws students into the period's material.

How does it work?

Sometimes it's a quick question. As I'm setting my World Lit texts on the podium, I turn to a group of kibitzing students and ask, "If Tartuffe were alive today, what do you think he'd be doing?" One kid blurts out, "I think he sold me that lemon I call a car." Surprised, another swears Tartuffe's a prominent shrink in California. Others claim they saw him last night preaching on the cable, begging for big bucks.

Sometimes it is a comment on relevant current affairs. For instance, about the time the news broke about President Clinton's alleged shenanigans with Paula Jones, I was teaching Racine's *Phaedra*. This potential scandal provided a great springboard for a lofty discussion on the effects of a public official's private morality—or lack thereof. "Ancient Greek city-states," decided one of my geo-politically-minded students, "aren't that far from Washington, D.C."

Sometimes it's a clever quotation or witty saying. Writing on the board Dorothy Parker's "You can lead a horticulture, but you can't make her think" provides quite an introduction to Guy de Maupassant's "Boule de Suif."

Sometimes it's a campus happening made fortuitous. On the day *The Scarlet Letter* provided the text, an itinerant preacher showed up in the student center courtyard, haranguing passing students as "Hell-bound sinners."

Sometimes it's a popular song. REO Speedwagon's lyrics "You're a candle in the window on a dark, cold winter's night" is a great lead for Poe's "To Helen." R. Kelly's "I Believe I Can Fly" helps a class on Updike's "Flight" take off.

Sometimes it's a reaction to a particular student or comment. Asking that gargantuan football player who is in the back row if he's ever considered the possibility of being injured—or worse—is a good segue into Housman's "To An Athlete Dying Young."

The Thirty-Second Strategem is a worthwhile experiment. Here are some hints on using it:

- **Make it quick.** (O.K., in some classes thirty seconds last five minutes).

- **Be casual.** Don't feel that every period you're a stand-up comic who's being paid to give your audience 60 minutes (or even 30 seconds) of your A material.

- **Keep it relevant**. Breaking the ice is important, but what's below the ice better be the day's lesson.

Charlie Sweet
Eastern Kentucky University

Openings

I try to open each class in a friendly manner and close in the same way. For example, on Monday, I might ask if anyone has an interesting weekend to tell about. This usually starts some good-natured bantering. I consciously strive for an open, friendly atmosphere in the class room.

Laura Denton
Maysville Community College

Entry Cards

In a developmental reading class I use an entry card for every class. On the first day the students write about their expectations for the class and ask any questions they may have about the class. I then use the cards to discuss the objectives and the syllabus in the class. Every class period begins with an entry card, but what the students write differs from day to day. One day I might use the entry card to give a pop quiz on a reading assignment; on another the students are asked to comment on something in their reading. Students can always ask questions on their cards. This anonymous (to the class, but not to the instructor) questioning frees students from the embarrassment of asking a question that they think everyone else knows the answer to. These cards sometimes take the class in an entirely different direction than I have planned, but this new direction is one that the students have indicated by their questions and comments is of importance and interest to the class. On some days the cards are useful in getting the class into a working mode and taking attendance while on other days the information on the cards may be the basis of discussion or other class work. Students who come late miss the points given daily for the cards.

Michele Freed
Lexington Community College

Short Answer Roll Call

To help build morale and comradeship within the class as well as set up the conditions for good class discussion, I like to have students introduce themselves instead of my calling out their names for roll call. This also facilitates receiving an extra bit of information from each student during the process. Fun extras include favorite flavor of ice cream, favorite sport, and so forth. Toward the end of the semester, roll call can also be used to get feedback on the course: favorite reading or topic, favorite activity, etc. This does not have to be done every class meeting, and students can be asked for input. Roll call can be done at the beginning, the middle or the end of class. It makes a pleasant change of pace beween activities.

George Brosi
Eastern Kentucky University

Current Events

A technique I've used from time to time to get my class off to a smooth start is to have students keep a close eye on the news. I award bonus points to students who find news items relevant to what we're studying on a given day. It's amazing how many times a story in the morning paper or a news magazine will deal with our material. For instance, a few terms ago we were discussing the revolutionary changes in world view brought about by Galileo and his contemporaries and the turmoil their theories caused when a student showed us a current newspaper clipping about the Vatican's official, if a bit tardy, pardon of the astronomer and reversal of its centuries-old position on the universe.

Anon.

Wake Them Up

In order to shake up my class and get them thinking about the day's lesson, I often dramatize the subject matter in an unexpected way. Once, for instance, to begin an argumentative section on prayer in public schools I opened the class by having the students stand, bow their heads and "join me in prayer." The discussion that followed was one of the most animated ones I've ever had.

Shirley Hayes
Eastern Kentucky University

It Works For Me

III. GETTING THE MOST FROM THE LECTURE

Traditionally the lecture has been the primary method of transmitting materials in the classroom. While current pedagogy suggests that other effective methods exist, most teachers continue to use the lecture extensively.

Unfortunately, many teachers seem to model their lectures on those pulled from an antiquated 1950's educational film. They stand rigidly behind the lectern reading a set of notes yellowed with age in a monotone designed to put even the most eager student to sleep.

Lectures, when handled creatively, can not only transmit material but also spark student interest and help promote a learning atmosphere in the classroom.

As you'll see, effective lectures involve more than knowledge of the subject and a pleasant speaking voice; getting the most from a lecture can call for strategies employing everything from visual aids to a good sense of humor.

The Quick Review

Each class period starts with a quick review of the major points from the last period. Then we proceed to briefly discuss that day's material and how it fits into the objectives currently being discussed. At the end of class (1-2 minutes), a review of that day's material is covered to tie in with the next assignment. This helps the student to tie in the day-to-day progress toward meeting class objectives.

Technique of Military Instruction

a. Tell them what you have told them (Review past material)

b. Tell them what you are going to tell them (Summary of present lesson)

c. Tell them (Today's lesson)

d. Tell them what you have told them (Review summary of today's lesson)

Paul Motley
Eastern Kentucky University

The Superstar Strategem

Ever watch the playoffs? The sport doesn't matter. No team gets to the championship if each player is absolutely equal. A superstar shall lead them, a player with superior abilities who puts the team on his/her shoulders and carries them to the trophy.

Occasionally your class might bog down and need a lift. One way you as teacher/coach can salvage this situation is to "create" a superstar. By this, I mean you deliberately choose for that day one particular student with whom you create a dialogue that you use to energize the class.

Let me illustrate. One day I was attempting to explain the structure of Neoclassic comedy, and the class was about as lively as a Tampa Bay Bucs crowd. Needing a way to jumpstart *mes etudiants*, I remembered that Ryan, buried in the middle of the room, had noted on his first-day 3x5 he was a Trekkie, so I suddenly asked him what the major set on the classic *Star Trek* was. As he described Captain James Tiberius Kirk sitting at the com in the center of the

Enterprise flight deck flanked by "Bones" McCoy and Mr. Spock, I drew the schematic on the board.

"What kind of advice does Spock always provide the Captain?" I asked Ryan.

"Pure logic," he said.

"And Dr. McCoy?" I pressed.

"'Do the human thing, Jim,'" Ryan said more confidently.

"So there's Kirk torn between reason and emotion," I translated to the rest of the class by pointing to my diagram, "just like the protagonist in our Neoclassic comedy."

"Yeah," said a voice from the crowd.

"So, Ryan," I continued, "what decision does Kirk make to save the Enterprise from the monster of the week?"

"He steers the middle course," said Ryan proudly, "sort of . . . moderation."

I resisted the temptation to shout "Eureka." Instead, I said, "Isn't moderation the lesson of every Neoclassic play?"

Obviously I don't select the same "superstar" to explain every lesson. Once I chose the class techno-nerd in Freshman English to discuss ethics and the computer. I've used older, non-traditional students who came from the business world to help me get through Kafka's criticism of the business mentality in *The Metamorphosis*.

What do I gain from this technique other than classroom variety? The superstar of the day has a moment of high self-esteem. The class, since a representative has contributed so much, feels actively engaged. A looser atmosphere, much more conducive to discussion, carries over from class to class. The pump has been primed, a good-natured competition has been created since other students wish to obtain superstar status, and we have all learned something about one of our members (plus a little knowledge).

Some Tips:

- On the first day of class, hand out 3x5 cards on which students list their hobbies, things they enjoy. Read these cards over and look for something you can use.

- Start by selecting extroverts, students who seem to be willing to contribute, students who don't mind being singled out.

- Keep the atmosphere light-hearted so that no one feels pressured.

- Be willing to come back to a superstar who has a successful performance.

- Beware that superstars like superstar treatment. They will come by your office, call you on the phone at home, and repeatedly speak out in class in an effort to maintain their exalted status. The up-side is that after a while you have a "straw person" about whom you can say things such as, "Lee insisted we have a quiz today" or "Lee was telling me before class that the reading assignments are too short."

- Give the superstar an easy win. Don't use minutia from the superstar's supposed field of expertise. Start with leading questions that can be easily answered and build the star's confidence. For instance, I once taught the pyramid of argument by analogizing it to a football team. "Who are those guys who play behind the defensive line," I asked the university's star cornerback, who resided in my back row, expecting the obvious "linebackers." "Guys too slow to play cornerback," replied my would-be superstar.

Hal Blythe
Eastern Kentucky University

Pop Allusions

Legendary football coach "Bear" Bryant once proclaimed, "Nobody ties to an English class." These days a lot of English instructors—as well as teachers in other disciplines—see the truth in that statement.

One of the most difficult things for an instructor to accomplish is to get students to leap the chasm from where they are in reference to the material to where the instructor wants them to be. A common, but usually unsuccessful solution is for the instructor just to present the material, hoping that the miraculous will happen—the student will suddenly see the light and make that great leap.

I've found an easy, more practical, and highly successful way of getting my students across that chasm. I constantly USE TOPICAL ALLUSIONS TO THE STUDENT'S WORLD. In simple terms, I make reference after reference to current media. The medium is the major message getting through to them, and the more I can relate my materials to their TV, movies, music, and sports, the better I reach them ("Reach out to me. I'll be there." [remember The Four Tops?]).

For instance, I was recently teaching a class about mammonism (materialism) during The Gilded Age, and I referred to the late 19th Century as the original

"Show me the money" generation, an obvious allusion to the clever catch-phrase in *Jerry Maguire*. Lately, to explain the Neoclassical use of rhymed heroic couplet, I start by asking about the usual rhyme scheme of rap music. We even put some lyrics from one of the current class favorites on the board. Then we chat about how the couplet is an attempt to impose order on the universe. Didactic literature always leaves its audience with a message, most often at the end, so I ask the class how the late, lamented TV show *Doogie Howser* always ended. Some tubeophile remembers Doogie sitting in front of his computer at the show's end typing on the screen what he learned from that week's episode. If a science class wanted to illustrate Galileo's struggles with his peers, they might point out what Stephen Hawking is going through with his contemporaries, or cite the famous episode of *Star Trek: The Next Generation* in which Hawking plays poker with such scientists as Data and Einstein.

Why should you make the effort to sprinkle pop allusions into your classes?

- Your material is made more accessible.
- Class interest perks up when you make your students feel secure with something they know.
- Respect for the instructor increases. They know you know the classroom material well, but well-placed allusions minimally create the illusion you know and care about their world (i.e. you're more than an ivory-tower egghead).
- Pop culture references are an easy entree. Most of us read the sports pages and/or entertainment section. We've even been known to channel surf and accidentally catch the machinations of malevolent Dr. Michael on *Melrose Place*.
- After a while you not only start to look for useful allusions, but your students begin to do the same. It's quite rewarding when someone tells you that forbidden love in *Phaedra* is just like what happened yesterday on her favorite soap opera.

Hal Blythe
Eastern Kentucky University

Cheap Visual Aids

In "The Purloined Letter" detective Dupin is able to retrieve the stolen letter and substitute a fake because he comes up with a quick technique for making a facsimile seal. Following Dupin's lead, I've developed a few makeshift props—cheap visual aids that have contributed to my classes.

Inspired by Dupin's example, I constructed for my Am Lit I class a letter holder in order to demonstrate the difficulty in Dupin's spotting the purloined letter from across the room. My materials were a used file folder, a ribbon from a gift a colleague had received, and a torn piece of duplicating paper.

To illustrate Fra Pandolph's fresco technique in "My Last Duchess," I usually use chalk to draw the smiling beauty on the plaster-covered concrete-block wall of my classroom. I've also used chalk to draw the outline of a dead body on the classroom rug. To point out the Rorschach-Test-like imagery in "The Love Song of J. Alfred Prufrock," I usually pour ink on file folders and hold the dried products up as ink-blot tests for my students.

Why go to so little trouble in the first place? What students visualize, they can remember. They usually get a good laugh out of my cut-rate props, and that relaxed atmosphere is also conducive to learning (it's interesting to note that in my end-of-the semester evaluations, they tend to recall these aids and rate them highly). Cheap visual aids also offer a nice change of pace from the formal lecture, and no matter how crude they are, they also demonstrate the old fuddy-dud has a certain amount of creativity.

Charlie Sweet
Eastern Kentucky University

The Parking Lot

At the beginning of every class period, I draw a circle in the corner of the blackboard. This is our "parking lot." Here I place questions or issues that need to be addressed but not at the time the student asks the question or raises the issue. This activity eliminates getting off track and ensures that I don't break the momentum of the current discussion or activity. You must allow time at the end of class to address "parking lot" questions to maintain credibility with the students.

Susan Edington
Madisonville Community

The On-Board Summary

Prior to each class period taught, I use a corner of the board to write up the main topics / ideas to be covered that period. This keeps the students more focused, and they know the progress through the class period.

Paul Motley
Eastern Kentucky University

Humor

I believe humor is an exceptionally important component of the teaching process. By humor, I don't focus on telling jokes—this is too stilted for me. I simply try to look at the light side of issues (as appropriate) or say things that are obviously outrageous to give students a chance to laugh and warm up to the subject a bit. I may also share stories, most of which are humorous, about experiences I've had as a student or nurse. Since I recently finished another degree, I still have fresh personal student stories. From my perspective this serves two purposes; humor helps the students remember the point made about the subject, and it helps students see me as human(e). I believe this is especially important in a profession with so much intensity, seriousness and competitiveness. I also believe it shows students that a person can be "professional" and humane at the same time. Obviously the timing is very important. I also look for cartoons to convey the relationship component of nursing—we're all in this together. Humor helps people keep their perspective about life, which can be a challenge in a profession like nursing—especially in the current practice arena.

Pam Moore
Eastern Kentucky University

The Reading Quiz

One policy that I've used for several years is fairly common, I think, yet in two ways is perhaps a little different: My quiz schedule in World Literature I and II as well as in American Literature II, American Romanticism and American

Realism. First, I give a short objective reading quiz over *almost every day's* assignment, including even the poetry. From the last third or half of the assignment I give three or four questions, each of which can be answered in a phrase or sentence, and ask the students to answer one of the questions. I try to make the questions reasonable ones—not overly difficult or "picky"—that a student who reads carefully might be expected to answer. Thus the students are quizzed over 90-95% of the required reading. Second, I count the cumulative quiz score forty percent (40%) of the semester grade. I feel such a heavy weight (actually the weight of two or three announced tests) is acceptable because the literature is the courses' reason for being, reading should be a major part of higher education, the students are considerably motivated by the quiz schedule to read the literature, and regular reading helps students better understand my lectures, take better notes, participate in discussion more easily, and of course learn more. In short, I believe that frequent quizzing and counting quiz scores heavily raise the educational quality of a course. I should add that I let the students drop three or four quiz scores, and often I give an extra-credit quiz over a play—sometimes two plays—produced during the semester by EKU Theater. (Using the plays is itself, I think, a very worthwhile educational activity, for it introduces students to a type of entertainment that they often do not know which is in turn often superior to commercial TV programs and popular movies; and they might well continue to enjoy live drama after they have left the university. A significant number of my students over the years have told me that they had never before seen a play, and that they intended to attend more play performances.) Students in evaluations have generally not complained about quizzes or their weight; more often they have tended to say quizzes helped them keep up with the reading, or that they considered the quizzes fair or reasonable.

Harry Brown
Eastern Kentucky University

The Advantages of Daily Quizzes

Some teachers never quiz their students, preferring other methods of assessment. Other teachers give pop quizzes, occasional questions about what the students read or studied in the previous meeting. I prefer the daily reading quiz.

When I first started teaching, I believed that whether or not a student read / studied an assignment was a matter of individual choice. Gradually I've changed

It Works For Me

my approach. Perhaps the chief impetus in my decision was a sad student who came to me at the end of a semester and told me he knew he was going to flunk my class. "But, Professor," he explained, "I want you to know I've read everything you assigned. Shouldn't that count for something?"

Yes, I agreed, it should. The next semester I instituted a daily reading quiz policy that accounts for 25% of each student's grade. Since that point, I've also discovered several advantages of giving between 25-30 quizzes/semester.

What is a typical reading quiz? Five factual questions that can be answered in a word or phrase. Taking less than five minutes of class time, the quiz is not devoted to interpretive questions (e.g. What is truth? Discuss the theme of "The Raven"). Rather I choose surface detail. With fiction I ask who, what, where, and when questions (e.g. In what country does *The Cherry Orchard* take place? How old is the main character, Sarty, in "Barn Burning"?). With non-fiction I choose bold-faced headings, italicized definitions, colored sidebars, bulleted information, or material from chapter summaries. If my students are willing to read the assignment, they should have an easy time answering my five questions. No background information or intellectual grasp of material is necessary.

Now, what are those advantages of daily quizzes?

- Students tend to actually read the material.
- Students show up for class on time since the quiz always comes first.
- Students are placed in the right attitude for learning.
- Students feel more confidant to discuss the material.
- Students raise their grades by simply reading the material.
- The start of class is signaled.
- The quiz provides a good lead-in for either a lecture or discussion of the material.
- Students grow curious about the answers. At the end of class (when the suspense is killing them), I usually answer any quiz question that didn't naturally pop up during class.
- The easy chance to do well gives students a feeling of self-esteem.
- 40 quizzes can be graded in about five minutes, and I don't feel a need to ask factual questions on tests just to see if they've read the material.
- Students are provided with a real foundation for intellectual growth (How can a student truly learn to interpret a work without knowing the facts? Note the case study method in law

school depends on the students first grasping the essential facts of the case).

Many options also exist with the daily quiz. To help raise the students' scores, you can give easy bonus questions. At the end of the semester you can drop a certain number of quizzes (e.g. a percent such as 10%). Extra credit work can fit in as a quiz score. You can test writing ability by insisting each answer be a complete sentence.

Charlie Sweet
Eastern Kentucky University

PPPPPP

In order to improve the organization of a class and to aid the students in note-taking, listing key terms on the chalkboard in the sequence of their presentation seems to work well. This technique also enhances the old adage "Prior Proper Planning Prevents Poor Performance (PPPPPP)." In addition, the teacher can glance at the board occasionally to maintain momentum, double check content, and avoid looking at notes as frequently.

Steve Fardo
Eastern Kentucky University

The Chapter Outline

I give a summary/outline of each chapter for students to study by; it lists the main points taken straight from my lecture notes. They know if it is on the hand-out, it is likely to show up on a quiz or exam.

Laura Denton
Maysville Community College

Grading Attendance

Unfortunately, getting students to class is often one of my most difficult jobs. To make this task easier, I've incorporated attendance into my grading formula.

Three points are given for each class attended; these points are put into the pool with the homework grades, the quizzes, and the exam grades. Receiving points just for showing up improves attendance.

Laura Denton
Maysville Community College

Building an Essay

Research tells us that our students learn much more from seeing than hearing. So, rather than lecture my students on how to build an essay, I give them this graphic. It makes very obvious that the general thesis can be supported by descending levels of generality right down to the specific examples. In one view my students can see the whole structure of a solid essay as well as the interdependence of the parts.

Building an Essay

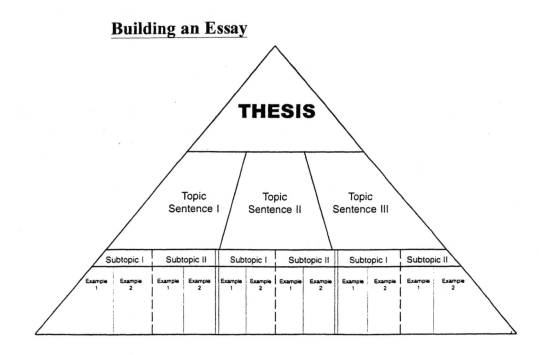

The Pillars of Civilization

In an attempt to teach my World Lit students that lit is not studied in a vacuum, I hand out this graphic at the beginning of the course. This diagram depicts the various pillars on which Western civilization has been based. Throughout the term I constantly refer to the various "pillars" of society that our literature challenges, upholds, or reflects during a specific age.

I find the graphic particularly effective during the 20th-Century discussions when seemingly all that has been valued in our civilization is being challenged. As a central reference point, the graphic makes fairly obvious what happens to civilization when the only pillar left supporting Western civilization is the INDIVIDUAL.

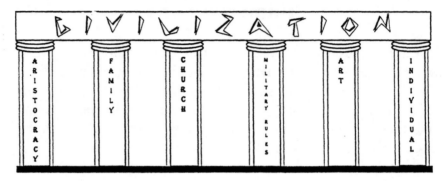

The Teaching Log

Before a course begins, I prepare a loose-leaf notebook with a page for each day of class. Each page has the same format with space to put notes ahead of time about what I would like to do that day and space to put notes after class on what actually happened. Dates can be put on each page easily using the computer. In the notebook after the basic page for the day I put copies of handouts I use that day so I can keep track of what handouts the students have already had.

Once I get into the course, I can see what activities I have already tried, and I can plan ahead what to do and what handouts to use. When I teach the course again, I can get a good idea of how I taught it last time.

George Brosi
Eastern Kentucky University

IV. DISCUSSION TECHNIQUES

Most teachers will agree that one of their most difficult tasks is getting students to discuss class materials. Sure, they'll chatter freely among themselves about last night's ballgame or the latest Counting Crows CD. But when the subject is Donne or Differential Equations, all talk ceases. They seem content to let the teacher ask then answer all pertinent questions.

Priming the student pump, especially in lower division courses, is difficult but not impossible. Below are a few tips from teachers who are not enamored with their own voices and have found ways to get their students to talk up.

Questioning Technique

In class discussions, I always try to ask high level questions (ones that demand more than facts to answer). One unique thing I do in question use in class is that I never answer my own questions. It has become a point of humor that I discuss during the first class period. I spread questions around and/or just wait until someone attempts to answer. This keeps the students attentive and into the class. I tell them if I just ask questions and then answer them, I don't need students. I can just go to the grill and question myself (over coffee).

Paul Motley
Eastern Kentucky University

My Visits to the Other Side

Because it was so difficult for students in our Psychosocial Nursing Class to really picture and understand many of the behaviors and characteristics exhibited by psychiatric clients, I decided a few years ago that I should "pull out the big guns." Once the basic concepts have been presented, i.e. concepts of mental health/mental illness, defense mechanisms, and principles of therapeutic communication, I arrive unannounced, of course, in full manic attire, brightly colored clothing, hair teased beyond the limits of its volume, a large brightly colored hair bow or scarf on top or closely attached at the side of my head, make-up beyond belief, including lipstick and lip liner slightly askew!

I "perform" the dialog of the day—it has never been the same thing twice, for about 10 minutes demonstrating the characteristics utilized by one in the manic state of bipolar disorder, characteristics that are often seen in those with other psychiatric disorders, such as flight of ideas, word salads, pressure of speech, delusional thinking, auditory hallucinations, and psychomotor hyperactivity. I then let the students know my "insanity" is over and continue with the lecture remaining in full "costume."

Students readily identify bipolar clients in the clinical sites as a result of this presentation and state it helps them more clearly understand the psychiatric clients they encounter. Although this theoretical information is important for their future practice in the health care field, I like to hope that the most important thing they learn for future reference is how to do your job while having fun.

Alicia Cook
Hazard Community College

The Alter Ego: A Technique for Priming the Pump

Have you ever felt really frustrated while teaching? You're doing your best to provoke discussion, but all you get in return are blank stares. So you ask a still-simpler question. Still no response. You reach a crossroads. You can move on to the next point, but you're determined to elicit some comment. How do you get them started talking? How do you prime the pump?

One solution I've found to be successful is a form of role-playing. Give in to that urge to answer your own question, but do it differently. Suppose you've just asked a key question, and the silence is overwhelming? Surprise your students by suddenly leaving the lectern and taking an empty seat in the classroom. Raise your hand, and say, "Dr. X, I've got an answer." Give it. Then walk back to the lectern, and thank your alter ego for that valuable insight. Then go find another empty seat and ask the lectern a question. You'll not only find you have a dialogue going between your persona as teacher and your alter ego as student, but gradually real students will participate.

Admittedly, this technique may seem a bit silly, but before you reject it out of hand, look what it accomplishes:

- Being different, the technique wakes up and stimulates the class.

- Once you invade students' space, they no longer feel secure in their silence.

- Once "one of their own" responds, the rest of the class is willing to join in the fun.

- Your alter ego allows you to pose questions students never do.

- Your alter ego speaks in their language, which makes the rest of the class feel part of the discussion.

- Your movement is kinetic. A body in motion tends to create other movement.

- The technique offers variety. Your student alter ego can either ask or answer questions. I've even sent my alter ego to the board. On one occasion, in sort of an exchange program, a real student wanted to move to the podium.

- It creates a more-open, fun-filled class atmosphere. You as teacher are perceived as having some ingenuity/sense of humor.

Hal Blythe
Eastern Kentucky University

Check With Your Neighbor

A technique that I use to keep students involved during a class period is "check-with-your-neighbor." During class I ask a question of the students, tell them to check with their neighbors, give them time to discuss the question, and then call on someone for an answer. I tell them that if the person I call on does not know the correct answer, his/her neighbor is in trouble. Rather than calling on an individual, if the answer is a one-word response I sometimes ask the class to respond as a group on the count of three.

Karl Kuhn
Eastern Kentucky University

What If Questions

In the past I have done historical "What If's" about how one event or cause and effect could be changed by, for example, John Wilkes Booth's gun misfiring. These hypothetical situations draw students into the discussion, stimulate them creatively, and get them to look more closely at the "real" event.

William Ellis
Eastern Kentucky University

V. GROUP ACTIVITIES / EXERCISES / FORMATS

How many times have you approached a task having prepared yourself by reading the instructions carefully and assembling all the needed tools only to find that once you started the actual assembly of that bicycle or hook-up of that computer the job didn't flow as smoothly as you'd have liked?

In the same way, students can often read the text, listen to the lecture, and even ask questions but still not have a solid hold on the class material.

Many effective teachers employ a "hands on" approach to class, introducing activities and exercises that call on students to participate actively in the acquisition of knowledge. Following are some strategies designed not only to engage student interest but also to foster student ownership of the materials.

Improv in the Classroom

I recently ran across an article in *Aikido Today* wherein Stephen Rentfrow talks about the relationship between improvisational comedy and Aikido. He lists the basic rules of each discipline, which I think can easily be applied to the instructor in the classroom:

- Trust (i.e. mutual respect between instructor and student)
- Don't negate or deny
- Don't ask questions (i.e. don't stop the action by asking for a detailed or memorized set-up)
- Make actional choices
- Make assumptions
- Give and take
- Listen, watch, and concentrate
- Work to the top of your intelligence

Mason Smith
Eastern Kentucky University

Visualizing Concepts

I have found that students comprehend and maintain concepts more fully if they can "experience" them. At the appropriate time I do a few unique things such as illustrate spatial concepts by letting students represent atoms and "act-out" reactions where so-called bulk effects influence reaction rates or product out-come. This visualizes the reaction and aids student comprehension.

When we discuss nuclear magnetic resonance (NMR), a statistical component to the absorption pattern for certain hydrogen nuclei must be explained. I will have students flip the proper combination of pennies (1-5) and tally the heads and tails that result. The statistical distribution of the coins will correlate reasonably well with the appropriate NMR absorption patterns, again aiding student comprehension of the concept.

John Meisenheimer
Eastern Kentucky University

An Experiential Illustration

I often use a kind of brief learning exercise as an experiential illustration. In order to illustrate how awkward it feels to change a behavioral habit, students are asked to observe what it feels like when they attempt to fold their arms differently, switching their top and bottom arms from their usual positions. Or, to illustrate that people are more influenced by modeled actions than verbal directives, I tell students to put their hands on their foreheads while at the same time I move a hand to my chin. To illustrate the behavioral effects of invasion of "personal space," I ask students to stand, move apart, and then slowly move toward another person until they are standing quite close, noticing all the while the effects on their feelings and behavior.

William Jones
Eastern Kentucky University

Illustrating Scenes

I sometimes have the students take 10 or 15 minutes to illustrate on paper particular scenes from works we have read. I find that having them visualize the scenes makes the setting, action and, most of all, the characters come alive. And, of course, their illustrations stimulate class discussion.

Ordelle Hill
Eastern Kentucky University

Acting Out Scenes

In my Shakespeare class, I have students form groups to act out a brief scene from one of the plays we study. They keep a record of all the decisions they make as they prepare to do the scene and submit an edited copy as a "support paper" for the scene.

This collaborative activity helps bring the students together while at the same time giving them another perspective (an insider's view) on the characterization, dialog, and movements of the scene. Their actual drama further helps other members of the class visualize the scene as well as stimulating discussion about the various interpretations.

Dominick Hart
Eastern Kentucky University

Describing a Martian

One of the first activities I always use in my ENG 101 class is to have students write a description of a Martian. I give them no guidelines as to length or content; they simply write a description of a Martian. The next class period, students exchange written descriptions and draw the Martian as described. They can add no detail or feature that is not given in their written description. Students share their drawings with the class. The importance of details and examples in writing is quite evident to them as they struggle to reconstruct a picture of the written word.

Susan Edington
Madisonville Community College

Special Person of the Day

Often in University classes, students feel lost and not an individual person, so I have instituted my *Special Person of the Day*. Early in the semester I give them a numbered list of all the students in the class. When the number opposite their name coincides with the assignment number, then they are "The Special Person of the Day." They may ask special questions, etc. It also helps me get to know them better. They must then turn in two copies of that day's assignment sheet. One copy is put in my office.

One student dubbed this "The Look Book." So this is its name. Then whenever another students misses a class, The Look Book may be checked out for reference. Often Special Persons say that when the test comes they do not have to study their particular section because they know it already.

Amy King
Eastern Kentucky University

The Student As Expert

At the beginning of the term in my World Literature classes I assign each student one work on which the student will become an "expert." I then ask each student to prepare, from his or her assigned work, four questions that can be directed to me. The questions can concern any aspect of the work, but for the most part they should relate to important matters such as theme, plot, characterization, philosophical implications, or cultural significance. The grade for this assignment is based on the student's apparent knowledge of the work (and writer) and on the quality of the questions. I find that assigning this in-depth coverage of at least one work for each student gives the students an opportunity to study a work much more thoroughly than they usually do in a survey class.

Ordelle Hill
Eastern Kentucky University

Phone Home

To help students get to the point in their news stories, I bring a phone to class and have them phone home. . .long distance. . .tell a parent what has happened in a particular situation which they have been assigned to cover. Invariably, what they say in this phone conversation includes the ingredients of a well-written lead for a news story. It's important to have the entire class listen in on the conversation; you can see the students finally come to understand the concept of focusing on the newsworthiness of the story. The exercise helps them write better leads.

Of course, this assignment could be appropriate in any class that demands attention to specific details. In a history class, for instance, the student could phone home the story of an historical event to see if he/she can present the event accurately. Or a student in a science class could "phone home" an experiment, trying to recount the exact step-by-step procedure.

Ron Wolfe
Eastern Kentucky University

Student Mentors

Students often make good teachers. Asking a better student to work with one who is struggling generally gives good results. Not only does the mentoring help the weaker student (sometimes students can explain concepts in terms easier for other students to understand), but the stronger student often gets a firmer grasp on the material by having to explain it in detailed fashion.

Laura Denton
Maysville Community College

The Process Theme

I often have students write what I call a process theme. In it they have to explain exactly "how to" do something. It can be anything they choose. . .how to bake a cake. . .do a flower arrangement. . .but they have to tell me exactly how it is done. Then, I have them bring all the props to class and as they read their papers, another class member is asked to follow their theme instructions exactly. What happens is they see that their instructions are not always clear. . .this opens the door to discussing ambiguity and similar problems in written communication. Plus, it is fun. (For example, one student wrote a paper on how to "make out" with a girl. The demonstration was. . .shall we say. . .interesting!)

Ron Wolfe
Eastern Kentucky University

A Made-To-Order Vocabulary Exercise

This freshman composition activity addresses two issues:
- understanding and practice of how dynamic, diverse vocabulary affects readers
- a chance to compose a document with a very tangible, "real life" application

1. Look up all possible synonyms of the verb "cook."

2. Write down definitions of individual synonyms to assure that you thoroughly understand the meaning of each word you will be working with.

3. Imagine that you own a small restaurant. Give it a name.

4. Compose a ten-item-long menu for your restaurant. Give each dish a title and a brief description. Make sure that your descriptions are as vivid and as detailed as possible. After all, you are in the unique position of implanting and manipulating the images that people create in their minds. Thus, they are more likely to order a dish that is "smothered with melted mozzarella cheese" than the dish which is "served with melted mozzarella cheese."

5. Your descriptions must not contain the word "cook." Use the synonyms instead.

6. There will be a contest for the best menu; the winner will receive a small prize.

Barbara Szubinska
Eastern Kentucky University

Building Well-Supported Paragraphs

While constructing paragraphs, writers must bear in mind that readers are at their "mercy" as far as how much information is conveyed to them. Therefore, it is best to assume that while constructing a paragraph, all the information possible about a given idea ought to be included. While it is hard to achieve such a distance while working with everyday concepts, the following exercise focuses on ideas and concepts known solely to the writer.

The teacher can either select a particularly obscure word or create one. I like the word "prehensile." Very few freshmen know what it means. I write the word on the board and ask students to speculate on what it might mean; in other words, we try to guess what part of speech it might be. Then, I ask students to choose an arbitrary meaning of the word and write a paragraph which will explain that meaning: either through description, narrative, comparison or contrast, etc. Students are not allowed to use a synonym to explain the meaning of prehensile.

After approximately twenty minutes, we read several of the definitions and comment on their merits. (Note: This exercise works very well in a computerized classroom where students have the ability to post texts to the entire class, such as Daedalus Integrated Writing Environment, MOO's or even e-mail.)

Barbara Szubinska
Eastern Kentucky University

Essay as a Collection of Paragraphs

Students often view writing an essay as a monumental and unmanageable task. The following exercise proves that composing an essay is similar to putting together a string of beads one at a time in which every paragraph is a well-rounded bead.

By now students should have mastered the art of composing paragraphs. I again use the word "prehensile" as a starting point. I disclose the meaning of the word and show a picture of a lemur with its prehensile tail. Then, I divide the class into groups of three to four people and ask each group to think of an innovation humans came up with because they observed something that animals or plants could do that their bodies could not. For instance, a crane that lifts heavy objects resembles a giraffe's neck. After a group comes up with an idea, they are asked to write a paragraph in which they include a detailed description of the innovation as well as the original phenomenon.

After groups are finished, they send their work to the instructor through whatever medium. They might also write it on the board. The instructor combines all the paragraphs and displays them on the board or screen.

Now, we have a rough draft of an essay. Later, the whole class provides suggestions on how to supply smooth transitions between ideas, unify the tone, add an introduction and conclusion, and proof-read the essay.

Barbara Szubinska
Eastern Kentucky University

The Interview

Here is an interesting assignment to introduce students to research. Conducting an interview is an easy form of research that makes them realize all knowledge is not archived in libraries or retrieved by computers. In addition, students learn:

- how to conduct an interview
- the importance of writing both now and in the future
- the relationship between oral and written presentations.

Interview a person who either works in the profession you are intending to join or a student in your major. Find out what kinds of writing the profession and/or major requires for you to master. How heavily does success in that discipline rely on the quality of your writing?

Be prepared to give a five-minute presentation of your findings. Bring samples unless issues of privacy of records prohibit it.

Barbara Szubinska
Eastern Kentucky University

Using Borrowed Material

One of the most difficult aspects of research for students to master is the incorporation of borrowed materials into their papers. Their problems begin with the age-old question, "What am I responsible for documenting in order to avoid plagiarism?" Then they must learn the various ways in which material can be taken from a source and used in their paper. And, finally, they need to be aware of the options open for actually melding the material into their text.

I've created a three-step approach (with handouts) that takes them from determination of what needs to be documented through the actual choices for incorporation of the material into the text. This information is appropriate for any level class in any discipline (note I do use MLA).

What To Document

Rules:
A. Do not document:
    1) your own ideas about what you read
    2) obvious facts from the reading
B. Do document:
    3) all quotations
    4) minor details
    5) all editorializing

Directions: For each of the following statements about "Cinderella," place in the blank the number of the reason that statement should or should not be documented.

    _____ 1. I think the Prince saved Cinderella in the nick of time.

    _____ 2. The eldest sister wanted to wear her French-trimmed, red velvet suit to the ball.

V. GROUP ACTIVITIES / EXERCISES / FORMATS   49

_____3. Cinderella was a young girl of "unparalleled goodness and sweetness of temper."

_____4. Cinderella and the Prince fell in love at the ball.

_____5. The sisters sent for the best tire-woman available, Mademoiselle de la Poche.

_____6. The stepmother is a jealous paranoid.

_____7. The godmother changed six mice into six horses, a rat into a jolly coachman, and six lizards into footmen.

_____8. In the end Cinderella forgives her sisters and finds them husbands.

_____9. The stepmother's major personality traits are pride and haughtiness.

_____10. Cinderella leaves the ball just before twelve.

_____11. The first persons to try on the glass slipper were the princesses and the duchesses.

_____12. When Cinderella asks to go to the ball, the sisters claim "it would make the people laugh."

_____13. Cinderella was a good counselor because she had excellent ideas, advised them for the best, and willingly proferred her services.

Quoting and Paraphrasing

I. The Original Quotation:

"Then, John LeCarre is concerned with espionage as one thread in the social fabric. No other spy writer I know has so meticulously delineated the chummy relationship between Oxford Dons and the British Secret Service."

II. The Direct Quotation:

Paul Henissart, a writer who believes John LeCarre the best writer of spy stories, explains, "No other spy writer I know has so meticulously delineated the chummy relationship between Oxford Dons and the British Secret Service" (307).

III. The Paraphrase:

Paul Henissart, a spy novelist in his own right, believes John LeCarre the best because he sees the English spy in relationship to English society, especially Oxford University (307).

IV. Excerpt Quoting:

Paul Henissart, who wrote *Narrow Exit*, finds John LeCarre's strength lies in the latter's insight into the English "social fabric" and particularly "the chummy relationship" between The Circus (British Secret Service) and "Oxford Dons" (307).

V. **Work Cited**:

Henissart, Paul. "Of Spies and Stories."
The Writer May 1980: 305-12.

Incorporating Quoted Material

- According to Dr. John Jones, noted chemist at Stanford University, "Marijuana smoking tends to alter the percentage of red corpuscles in the blood" (153).

- In "Marijuana and the Blood," Dr. John Jones makes a rather shocking statement about marijuana's effect on the blood: "Marijuana smoking tends to alter the percentage of red corpuscles in the blood" (153).

- In "Marijuana and the Blood," Dr. John Jones says, "Marijuana smoking tends to alter the percentage of red corpuscles in the blood" (153).

- In "Marijuana and the Blood," Dr. John Jones suggests that "Marijuana smoking tends to alter the percentage of red corpuscles in the blood" (153).

- "Marijuana smoking," says Jones, "tends to alter the percentage of red corpuscles in the blood" (152).

- "Marijuana smoking tends to alter the percentage of red corpuscles in the blood," says Dr. John Jones in "Marijuana and the Blood" (153).

Anon.

Collaborative Group Work

In recent years I have discovered the effectiveness of collaborative group work. This group structure, however, must be organized carefully to be most productive. I especially like electronic discussions employing the group dynamic. For example, I might take my class to the computer lab to use Daedulus' *interchange* for a group discussion. In order to make sure that discussions move along smoothly, I have each group choose a group leader. The group leader makes the decision when a question has been discussed adequately and moves the discussion on to the next question. To make sure that each group is adequately discussing each question, I monitor the discussion, and when I think the group needs help, I enter the discussion. In addition, I explain to the class that their discussions will be saved on the LAN so that I will have a permanent record of them. (The most important part of the electronic discussion is the group leader. Before I had the groups choose leaders, the discussions appeared to be more chaotic).

To facilitate group organization and operation, I have developed an instruction sheet I give to each student offering some tips.

Collaborative Group Work

1. Be sure to exchange phone numbers and schedules. Remember that the group can expect to meet at least once outside of class times.

1._____	4._____
2._____	5._____
3._____	6._____

2. Each person in a group is expected to participate equally in the collaborative assignment.

3. Group time should be used to work on the collaborative assignment. Other appropriate use of group time includes discussing assignments, difficult readings, or problems concerning class assignments. (Remember gossiping is not an appropriate use of group time).

4. Prioritize how group time is to be used. For example, be sure to accomplish the immediate assignment before discussing assignments that are not part of the current assignment.

5. If the group has a question concerning any class assignment or reading, this is a good indication that the instructor should be approached for help.

6. When a group presentation is being prepared, be sure the group understands the assignment. Then divide the work fairly. Before the presentation, the group should get together and practice. (Grades will be given for individual and group work on group presentation).

7. Everyone is responsible for taking notes during collaborative group time since everyone is responsible for knowing information and assignments given and discussed during group meetings.

Linda Doerge
Eastern Kentucky University

Role-Playing in Group Learning

One experiential approach to presenting group functions is to have five or six students role-play as group members in the initial meeting of a student committee assigned a specific task, such as writing rules for student elections. As preparation for role-playing, I privately assign each participating student a different role. Some are assigned leadership roles, such as "initiating," "clarifying," and "gatekeeping," while others are assigned dysfunctional roles, like "playing." Since these individual roles are assigned confidentially, no one knows anyone else's role or the role's probable effect on the group's productivity. Students not in the role-playing group sit in a large circle, or "fishbowl," surrounding the role-playing group and carefully observe without comment what happens during the meeting.

Following the activity, I assist the students through the learning cycle toward the objective of understanding group leadership. Facilitation is accomplished primarily through my raising appropriate questions. For example, I could initially ask the role players (and later, the students in the outside "fishbowl") what they experienced during the activity, encouraging the students to identify and share as much experiential data as possible, including emotions, thoughts, and perceptions. In response to these questions, students might report, for example, experiencing relief when someone finally suggested an agenda for the meeting, feeling affirmed when another group member encouraged their participation and then wanting to contribute to the group's success, or being irritated by a group member's constant joking. Here my questioning helps students become aware of experiential data by *observing* their previous *experiences*.

William Jones
Eastern Kentucky University

The Personalized Pop Quiz

I call all my in-class graded assignments "pop quizzes," and one of my favorite ones gives students an opportunity to redo exactly the parts of an earlier assigned paper which need revision. Here is how it works. As I am grading an assigned paper, I simply have a blank sheet of paper at my side. At the top I put: "Personalized Pop Quiz" along with the student's name and the date. As I notice problems with the paper or opportunities to do better, I number and write down requests that the student redo or correct part of the paper. One of my favorites is "Write the 'it' out of the second sentence in the third paragraph." What I mean is to rewrite the sentence so that it does not depend upon the use of "it" as a pronoun whose antecedent is not clear until the whole context is considered.

This idea has worked exceptionally well. Students are directed to work on their own peculiar deficits or opportunities. After doing the Personalized Pop Quiz, the student will basically have a new draft of the paper reflecting extra effort where it is most needed. Some students have further to go and will have to work harder than others on the quiz, but all students will be given a challenge appropriate to their level. For example, "Rewrite the fourth paragraph with more dynamic verbs," or "Pretend you are on a debate team taking the opposite position as you advanced in the paper, but a spy gave you this paper from the opposing team. Briefly sketch what arguments you would use to supersede the ones given in this paper." This technique is especially effective for the first few papers required.

George Brosi
Eastern Kentucky University

Public Conferencing

The second time a writing class meets, I like to read several student papers out-loud to the class. If the class is long, wisdom suggests reading them after the break so that the embarrassingly poor ones can be avoided and the striking ones can be included for sure. As the papers are read, I interrupt them with comments about structure, word-choice, grammar, indeed about every aspect of writing. I am sure to be abundant in my praise and polite in my suggestions for improvement.

When students know that their papers are likely to be read to the entire class, they tend to put more into them. This also serves as a reminder that a good way to proofread a paper is aloud. Reading papers in class insures that the teaching is in response to real needs, not an obscure abstract need the instructor feels. When the first assignment is a humorous narrative essay, this teaching technique also helps insure good vibrations for the course.

George Brosi
Eastern Kentucky University

The Circle Critique

On the day when a draft is due of a one-page assignment, have the students sit in one big circle—honest, I have done this even in a lab room and an auditorium. Then have the students pass their drafts around the circle either clockwise or counterclockwise (somehow I prefer counter!). My favorite assignment for this activity is the resume, and I sit in the circle and pass my resume along with the rest. Students are encouraged to write on the papers, even to contradict the reactions of students who wrote on the papers earlier. After most students appear to be done, I ask them to pass the papers again, whether or not everyone is finished. For the resume, I get faster and faster, since one of the values the resume-writer attempts to achieve is to impress the reader who is merely leafing through a big stack. Eventually all students get their resumes back with lots of helpful comments.

George Brosi
Eastern Kentucky University

Double Discussion Groups

Do you want students to be productive during small discussion group gatherings? Here is a suggestion: Have the students count off by double numbers: 1-1, 1-2, 1-3, 1-4, 2-1, 2-2, 2-3, 2-4, 3-1, 3-2, 3-3, 3-4, 4-1, 4-2, 4-3, 4-4. Tell them that for the first half of the class the groups will be formed based on the first number and that for the second half of the class the groups will be formed on the basis of the second number. Magically the dynamics have been manipulated so that none of the students will have a single one of the sample people in their second group as were in their first! This means that each student will have to take notes on what is done in the first group in order to take the information to the second group!

Yes, I've tried having small group discussion with and without this safeguard and been amazed how much more is accomplished when every student in the room knows that no other member of the first group will be in the second.

George Brosi
Eastern Kentucky University

Student Samples

At the end of each semester I pass out permission slips to all the students asking for their permission to use all of their papers as I see fit so long as I white-out their names. Students are assured that I will get enough permissions to not be adversely affected by anyone who is uncomfortable giving permission, and they are not asked to sign the slip until after I have told them their grade for the course. I assign each student a number and then white out the names and replace them with numbers.

The next semester I can make copies of any paper to show my new students a real-life sample of how a student last semester did the assignment. Sometimes I copy A-D papers on an assignment so students can know what kind of grade to expect for their performance and what makes me lower and raise grades. I never let the students spend much time looking at the samples—just enough to get the general idea. Usually I have several examples and only a few copies of each, so students have to keep them moving and get them back to me. I always do a count so I know that nobody stashed away an A paper—or a D one for that matter!

Students LOVE this idea! It really helps minimize the "I don't know what he wants" whine! I have also done assignments myself and passed them around as models, but that does not work nearly as well as this. Somehow students figure I can do my own assignments. They feel better knowing that last semester's students can complete my assignments satisfactorily.

George Brosi
Eastern Kentucky University

Shared Research

To make my section on the research paper more meaningful, I have students write on the same general topic with similar theses. I find this strategy effective for several reasons:

- My lectures and examples are relevant to every student, improving student discussion and interest
- Students can work together more easily sharing research and ideas
- The class develops a "communal" notebook (on reserve in the library) with copies of each student's research
- Students with opposing viewpoints can bounce ideas off each other
- Class discussion is more meaningful since everyone is dealing with the same basic material

Because the main goals for my students are the ability to develop and support a sound thesis and improve general writing skills, I do not want them to bury themselves in the library or on the Internet. This shared assignment meets my needs.

Shirley Hayes
Eastern Kentucky University

Developing Perspective

For a lesson in perspective, the following may be helpful:

a. Bring in a medium-sized statue or stuffed animal, etc. (The more the features, colors, etc., the better). Place the object on a desk in the front of the room.
b. Have the students describe exactly what they see from where they are sitting.
c. Divide the students into groups of three's—from each side and the middle. Have them read what they saw and discuss the differences.

Shirley Hayes
Eastern Kentucky University

Building A Poem

For a class experimenting with poetry writing, the following exercise can help generate some ideas:

a. Locate advertisements, flyers, magazines and cut out nouns, adjectives, adverbs, and strong verbs.

b. Take 25 or so and make a poem that uses many or most of the words. Also, the entire class could have a "pool" of 50 or so words and see what types of poems emerge from the same words.

Shirley Hayes
Eastern Kentucky University

VI. CLOSURE

Just as the first few minutes of class can help insure the success of the entire hour, so the closing minutes can accomplish a great deal for the effective teacher. Rather than running the class till the bell, asking for questions that you don't have time to answer (and hurried students won't take time to ask), gathering your material and rushing from the room, use the end of the hour judiciously.

When used effectively, the final minutes of class can allow you to summarize major points, ascertain student understanding of the lesson through comments and questions, and preview the next session. Further, a leisurely, prepared-for close of class encourages students to chat with you and each other.

Here are a few suggestions for successful closure from teachers who realize the importance of finishing each class session strongly.

Closing Activity

As a closure activity, let students develop two or three possible test questions based on the material covered in the day's class. You will know if the students comprehended the material, you will know what came across as the major points to the students, and you will know what material needs further clarification or explanation. If you actually use some of the students' questions on upcoming tests, students will be quite motivated to engage in this activity!

Susan Edington
Madisonville Community College

Review and Preview

Some of the most important minutes I spend in any class session are those at the very end. I never really think of this time so much as closure as I view it as a chance to tie things together and project upcoming materials.

At times my "closure" period consists of reviewing the day's material, tying it to what we've done in previous classes and suggesting how this lesson will link with the next. If a particularly difficult lesson is coming up, however, I like to do a little more with the closing minutes. For such lessons I actually "preview" the upcoming material, giving hints for handling specific "tough spots" and warning students if extra time will be needed for exercises.

My students seem to like this "preview" and actually become comfortable asking questions in response to my comments. For such preview sessions I always reserve a few extra minutes for my closure.

Marsha Blythe
University of Kentucky

Student Summaries

Students often sit through class sessions, listening, taking notes, even asking questions and making comments, but at the session's end they really don't have a firm grasp of the material as a whole. In order to gauge their comprehension, I reserve a few minutes at the end of class in which I ask students to summarize the day's material in a paragraph emphasizing what they perceive as the main points.

These paragraphs allow students a chance to put together the day's material while it's fresh in their minds while also giving me an insight into how well they're grasping my presentation and just what aspects they think are most important. Because they know the paragraph's coming, students pay closer attention in class and tend to take better notes. I even use their paragraphs at times to launch the next session's discussion.

William Jones
Eastern Kentucky University

Student Questions

Teachers are fond of saying that the only bad question is the one not asked. So that my students won't fall prey to their shyness or a lack of time during discussion, I set aside the last portion of class to give them a chance to ask questions.

After summarizing the day's material, I have students jot down two questions they'd like to ask about the material. Of course, I get many simple questions on factual material. Often, however, I have been surprised at the depth of some of the questions and have used the questions as "openers" for the next class.

In addition, the questions give me an indication of how well I'm coming across to the students.

Anon.

Closing Quiz

Many teachers open their class with a quiz over the assigned readings in order to make sure students are keeping up with the material. I like to give a brief quiz at the end of class to be sure students are getting the material presented. In the last few minutes of class I ask a series of short answer questions over the session's material. Students can use their notes; all questions come from lecture/discussion rather than readings.

This quiz encourages students to be on time for class, to be attentive, to take clear notes, and to ask questions if material is not understood.

Hal Blythe
Eastern Kentucky University

———————

VII. CHOICE ASSIGNMENTS

Effective teachers realize that much of the learning in a semester goes on outside the classroom. As a result, they design assignments that reinforce the materials presented in class as well as encouraging students to investigate further on their own.

Such assignments, rather than being a drudgery for students, can provide avenues for student individuality and often lead to more lively class participation next session.

Below are some choice assignments that have worked to whet student interest and promote class participation.

Applying Psychology to Life

In my Psychology course, I ask students to develop a project which applies a psychological concept to a real life situation. A project plan is submitted profiling what will be done, why they are interested in this topic, and what psychological concept is applicable to the project. Students present their projects to the class toward the end of the semester. Students are encouraged to use media in their 10 minute presentation.

I have had great success with this assignment. Examples of projects would be:

- token economy system used on children
- assessment of violence depicted in cartoons
- memory techniques
- case studies on bulimics
- stress contracts

I believe it makes the material come to life and shows the significance of it to our lives.

Arlene Alexander
Henderson Community College

What's Your Style?

Ask students to bring tapes of their favorite recording artists. Anticipate genres that may not be represented, such as classical, chant, etc. Ask students to brainstorm what distinguishes a particular style of music, and write their suggestions on the board. (My students usually mention beat, lyrics, themes, instrumentation, vocalists, etc.) Then play one piece from each selection and ask students to describe what they hear, noting distinctive characteristics of each style. Call on several students to read their descriptions. Note how various subjects seem to be appropriate to a certain style of music. For example, love songs are often country or blues, but rarely rap. Patriotic songs frequently feature percussion, etc. Then discuss how these details of style translate to writing. For example, a country song has many of the same stylistic features found in a ballad. Students should see that writing styles vary according to purpose and audience, and that diction translates to lyrics, sentence variation to rhythm, and so on.

Sandy Cavanah
Hopkinsville Community College

Submitting for Publication

A requirement that I include in English 804: Seminar in Creative Writing: Poetry, as well as in independent studies in writing poetry, the idea for which I received from Professor Emeritus of English J. Walter Nelson, is to have students submit their poetry for publication. Each student in English 804 at the end of the semester turns in, along with all writing—notes, drafts, notebook entries, etc.—done during the course, all poems she/he considers finished. The poems are to be divided into groups of two or three and put in addressed envelopes, one group to an envelope, along with SASE, ready to be submitted for publication. (I look at the submissions and then put them in the mail.) I suggest some magazines that students might submit to—usually Kentucky or regional literary magazines, poetry magazines, or student publications, or magazines that are fairly new and thus less established and less competitive for submitting writers; and of course the students can themselves find magazines to which they can send their poems. In the very few times I have taught English 804, over half the class have published at least one poem written during the semester. And just this week a student with whom I worked this past semester in an independent studies course came by the office to tell me she has had accepted one poem (from some five or six submissions) to be printed in a broadside. She has not yet heard about the other submissions. Submitting for publication connects the classroom experience with the outside world—makes writing more practical and real—and of course publication is very exciting for the students (as well as for their instructor!), giving them added confidence in themselves and their work.

Harry Brown
Eastern Kentucky University

Reading Report

A simple but effective strategy I have used in recent years, primarily in upper-division courses, requires that students turn in a brief report for **each** reading assignment. The report consists of two components: (a) a statement about what the student believes is the **most important argument** in that reading, and (b) a **question** the student has about the reading that he/she would like me to discuss in class. Students tell me this type of assignment "encourages" them to keep up with their reading. It also provides the instructor with numerous lecture and discussion opportunities related to a particular reading assignment. Students seem to listen a little more carefully when I am answering one of their classmates' questions.

Paul Blanchard
Eastern Kentucky University

Academic Limericks

I have stimulated some creative abilities by providing a small amount of extra credit for students writing organic chemistry limericks. The best one submitted should not be read in mixed company.

John Meisenheimer
Eastern Kentucky University

The Cultural Report

One addition to the traditional classroom that I've come up with for my World Lit class is the ACE, the Alternative Cultural Experience. I give my students two periods "off" (which come during "dead" week); in return they contract to attend two outside cultural activities and write a report on each. These cultural events include our annual culture festival, foreign films (the Foreign Language Department and the library show them), university and community drama, art exhibits, concerts, and the like.

Why do I do it? I spend sixteen weeks teaching about other cultures, but they are mainly viewed through the medium of print. I feel my students have a tendency to be insular and the exposure to the "prima facie" culture will broaden them. Whether they taste poi for the first time, hear a Chinese lecturer talk about her religion, or experience the Japanese sense of honor that would demand suicide for certain occasions, they learn something. And they have to write about it, which forces them to think about what they encountered. I also ask them to somehow relate their experience to the course content.

Some student evaluations have reluctantly admitted how they started out hating the assignment but realized poi "isn't half bad." By limiting their choice of subjects in the beginning (e.g. Jackie Chan movies don't count), I can usually expose them to something of educational value.

Cultural Report

1. **RATIONALE: you have contracted to attend several cultural alternatives to the traditional classroom experience.**

   a. You must go to a minimum of two separate events.
   b. All events must be acceptable to the instructor.
   c. During the semester the instructor will provide a list of such events. If you wish to use non-listed events, you must clear them with the instructor.
   d. Since the ability to communicate is a necessary skill at all levels of university work, you must provide a written report for each event.

2. **FORM: for each event attended, you will be expected**

   a. To include a Title Page (title of your report, your name, section, and date).
   b. To use standard English.
   c. To write clear and coherently related sentences.
   d. To organize your entire report as well as individual paragraphs in meaningful patterns.
   e. To provide specific support for your individual ideas.
   f. To document where appropriate using the style adopted by your major or MLA.

g. To include when necessary certain addenda (e.g. ticket stub, Bibliography, program).

3. **COMPONENTS:**

a. Identify the cultural event (who, what, where, when, how long).
b. Specify the medium (e.g. film, play, slide show).
c. Summarize the event.
d. Appraise the event (e.g. did you understand it, did you think it was clearly presented)
e. Describe how you think the event has enlarged your understanding of Western culture.

4. **REMINDERS:**

a. All reports are due two weeks before the semester ends.
b. Un-turned-in reports will be treated as double cuts.
c. Turned-in reports will aid positively in the determination of borderline grades.
d. Say what you really believe, not what you think the instructor wants to hear.

Hal Blythe
Eastern Kentucky University

Reading Guide

In any class students can benefit from a guide to help them better understand their readings. I've come up with a series of questions and a short writing assignment that work to draw students to specific considerations that clarify often difficult materials.

Before Reading:

1. Considering the title, what do you expect the reading to be about?
2. What opinions do you hold on this subject?

3. What do you know about the author? What expertise does the author have that relates to this subject?

Reading:

1. Who is the author's audience?
2. What is the main point of the reading?
3. What details does the author use to support this point?
4. What information or details does the author give in the first paragraph?
5. What is the author's attitude toward the subject? What details does the author give to support this attitude?
6. How is the reading organized? (Think of how it could be outlined.)
7. Does the author use figurative language? If so, how?

After Reading:

Write a 1-1/2 page journal entry in which you speculate about what the author intends readers to think about the reading's subject. As you write, be sure to summarize the main points of the essay, as well as quote phrases and sentences that support your ideas.

Linda Doerge
Eastern Kentucky University

The Mini-Casebook: A Successful Exercise

What is a mini-casebook? It's a self-made booklet of around 15 pages containing both primary and secondary sources on a specific subject. Although I have produced several such works, I have created one that seems more successful than the rest.

First, I had to choose a subject that all my freshmen knew and had no major-oriented advantage. What are teenagers most interested in? What do they talk about? What do they spend their spare time and change on? After nixing sex and drugs, I found the answer was as close as the nearest student lost in a Walkman world.

ROCK.

I started surveying the songs of the modern rock era (I grew up in) for tunes whose lyrics offered more interpretive possibility than "Gliddy gloop gloopy,/Niney noop noopy,/La la lo lo." One blast from the past stood out. In 1971 Don McLean had sung a 7 and $\frac{1}{2}$ minute cut whose chorus my generation knows by heart. The lyrics of "American Pie" won out over the Beatles and Simon & Garfunkel.

Then I started the research to put together the actual booklet. Part I of the casebook was McLean's actual lyrics. Part II was a collection of secondary sources that included an excerpt from a book, some newspaper pieces, and several articles from popular magazines. The final product, *The "American Pie" Casebook*, yielded several advantages.

First, some minor points. It doesn't favor one student major over another (e.g. the English major writing on Milton's sources). It isn't about subjects with which the majority have little interest (e.g. Salt Licks in Early Kentucky) or little background (e.g. animal rights), and it doesn't provide a confrontation with a subject on which the professor has a strong viewpoint (e.g. abortion).

Next, by initially providing the student with some sources, the mini-casebook approach gives them a head start on research. I also require interviews, library research, and surfing the Internet, so the variety prevents them from over-relying on a single source (most students come to class thinking research means copying their *Funk & Wagnalls* or computerized *Grolier*).

The brevity and accessibility of this casebook nips intimidation in the bud. For students who are overwhelmed by the maze of library stacks and the World Wide Web, 15 pages doesn't seem half bad. To make the assignment less intimidating in scope, I restrict their focus on McLean's song to six topics: the use of the chorus, the religious imagery, political commentary, the value of rock to McLean, images of loss, and McLean's past vs. his present in the song. I have reduced the scope to these topics because I have found they are concrete enough (e.g. More than "Themes in 'American Pie'") and I know the sources exist out there to do good research.

Unlike research projects that demand simply an accumulation of facts and figures, "American Pie" lends itself to unlimited interpretation (I'd call it "literature," but that would scare my students off). Since McLean's song is built around undefined phrases like "Miss American Pie" and "The day the music died," students are encouraged to offer their own insights drawn from both their readings of the lyrics and secondary sources. Furthermore, not one of the secondary sources available gives a complete treatment of one of my assigned topics. In short, my students can become experts on their subject.

I avoid negative reinforcement by asking for no more than 1000 words on the student's chosen topic. This brevity allows the student to double check each entry as well as the grammar. I've even experimented with having the students write the entire paper from note cards during two successive class periods in which I'm always available to answer specific questions.

Because I identify the primary source, provide a limited amount of secondary sources, and give students only six choices of topics, I control the project. Over the past few years it's been fairly easy to keep up with everything written on "American Pie."

This control allows me to prevent most plagiarism. As far as I know, no term paper service has touched on these restricted topics. Additionally, since my students write in class from notes I've checked over a couple of times, plagiarism is doubly difficult. Furthermore, because I've kept up with the sources (something my students know), I'm certain no student has tried to pass off some critic's viewpoint as his/her own.

Even with large comp classes, grading is kept at a minimum. Since I usually don't have to pause in the middle of a paper to check the exactitude of a quotation, its source, or the page number of a given article, I am able to pay more attention to what the paper says, its structure and logic, its mechanics. Because I can handle the first grading so quickly, I have time for students to revise.

As far as I'm concerned, the Casebook has been as easy as pie. The basics of research and the structure of such a paper are hidden under an entertaining crust. I recommend you try a slice or bake your own as I've done with many other topics.

Charlie Sweet
Eastern Kentucky University

The Editorial Cartoon

An editorial cartoon can be adapted for any in-class writing assignment. In addition to using it as a diagnostic, I have also used the cartoon as a means for discussing description, organizing, symbolism, etc. The editorial cartoon can be used easily for an in-class writing but several things need to be remembered when choosing a cartoon. These things are: 1) currency, since the most interesting news is recent news, 2) enough details to provide adequate text for a writing, and 3) a cartoon about an event with which all the students will be familiar or at least able to interpret adequately for the assignment.

Linda Doerge
Eastern Kentucky University

Using the Computer for Research

I've developed a handout that can be used for teaching computer skills relevant to composition and research. If a school has a problem with 25 or so students going to the same location (e.g. *Yahoo*), then the activities can be staggered by having each group begin with a different activity. These particular activities are directed toward our capabilities at EKU, but the activities could be generalized. I've given fairly general goals, not the step-by-step process for achieving these goals. I give separate detailed instructions to my classes.

Using the Computer for Research

There are several activities given for today. In order to avoid problems with too many computers trying to go to the same place, each group will begin with a particular activity. Find your group in the following list and begin with the assigned activity. Your group should spend about 15 minutes with each activity before moving on to the next activity. Answer the questions given for each activity on a separate sheet of paper.

GROUP 1 will begin with Activity 1; GROUP 2 will begin with Activity 2; GROUP 3 will begin with Activity 3; GROUP 4 will begin with Activity 4; GROUP 5 will begin with Activity 5.

ACTIVITY 1: Send students to the campus library for author/title/periodical searches.
ACTIVITY 2: Send students to do the available Internet resources through browsers.
ACTIVITY 3: Send students to research newspapers through the Internet.

ACTIVITY 4: Send students to research popular news magazines on the Internet.

ACTIVITY 5 : Send students to research the instructor's homepage on the Internet.

Linda Doerge
Eastern Kentucky University

Talking About Writing

On the day students have a writing assignment due I have them talk about what they have written (Tell the class). Not only does this presentation stimulate class interest and discussion, but also it makes the students more careful with their writing (both what they've said and how they've said it).

Judy Steinbach
Eastern Kentucky University

An Emotional Response

Read something with emotional appeal or shock value—hopefully something that has a direct relationship to the students' lives (This semester I read about a chemical leak.). Have them start their journal responding in writing to the brief class discussion that follows the reading.

This assignment both draws students into the class discussion of the reading and makes them think more deeply on an emotional subject about which they've probably only felt (e.g. racism, child abuse, drugs).

Judy Steinbach
Eastern Kentucky University

The Time Capsule: An Exercise

Need a different way for your class to grasp a general principle? Are you tired of just writing key definitions on the board and watching your students' eyes glaze over because the notion is too complicated or too abstract? Do you want to make your class think?

Why not let them arrive at the definition themselves?

One method I've found useful in World Lit is The Time Capsule. To help my students understand Neoclassicism, I "dig up" a capsule from the 18th Century. In it is a picture of an English formal garden, an architect's rendering of a typical estate, and Arthur Murray-like footprints of two couples doing the minuet. I ask my students what these forms have in common. The students easily pick up the balance, the symmetry. What, I ask, do these patterns reveal about the people who produced the forms?

Other possible uses of this method abound. In American History or Current Sociology, you might unearth a time capsule for 1992 in which the comic book event of the year was the death of Superman, two of the highest-grossing movies were *Batman Returns* and *Lethal Weapon III*, and the top-rated TV show was *Roseanne*. What do these three pop culture expressions reveal about the opening of the 90's in our country?

You can also "discover" the safe-deposit box that belongs to Sigmund Freud or Marie Curie. You might work the exercise two ways. After studying Madame Curie, you can ask the class what they'd find in the lock box, or on day one of studying Curie you can tell them what's in the box, then ask what her personality was like.

Why bother with the Time Capsule approach rather than rely on the traditional lecture?

- Being different, the approach (i.e. non-lecture) creates interest.
- Whether inductive or deductive, everyone loves a mystery.
- It draws students into the discussion.
- It forces students to think rather than being passive receptors.
- The exercise fosters student ownership of the principle since they're the ones who establish it.

Hal Blythe
Eastern Kentucy University

WIT Sheets

To encourage students to read literature assignments thoughtfully, I have designed a one-page form I call a WIT Sheet. WIT is an acronym for Wonder, Interpret and Tie-in. Each of these three parts of the form has two sections with the second section requesting support from the text of the assigned work properly documented. "W" asks what the student wondered about the work. This is a request for a rudimentary research question. "I" asks for an interpretation. This is a request for a rudimentary thesis statement. "T" asks for a tie-in from reading, viewing or personal experience. Filling out the form gives students practice asking pertinent questions, finding answers to them and connecting literature with life. Filling out the "because" part of each of the three sections gives students practice in documentation. I grade the WIT Sheets exactly as I would a research paper, giving students practice in using first and last names, avoiding first and second person, writing in the present tense and active voice and other conventions of university-level writing. Of course, I also grade down for mistakes in grammar and punctuation.

George Brosi
Eastern Kentucky University

Assignment Choices

If I plan, for instance, to assign five papers in the semester, I like to have seven paper assignments in the syllabus, making sure that students realize only five are required. This gives students willing to do extra a chance to do so, and it also gives some leeway so that students don't have to ask to be excused or late with an assignment. This also means that I am not grading a paper for every single student on every assignment date.

George Brosi
Eastern Kentucky University

VIII. TESTING

Ideally, tests would not be necessary. Students would work diligently, and everyone would master the class material. But experience suggests that college classes are far from ideal. Most students need, even desire, that tangible proof that they have learned the material presented.

Tests, however, don't need to be foreboding instruments of torture designed more to find out what students don't know than what they do. Handled effectively, tests can be a true measure of student mastery of material and can even function as a tool for further learning.

Following are a few suggestions for making your tests positive experiences for you and your students.

Preparing for Examinations

I've found this advice (which I hand out to students early in the term) particularly effective in helping them prepare for exams.

It is extremely important for you to prepare for examinations properly so that you will not be rushed and tired on examination day. All textbook reading and lecture note taking and revision should be completed well ahead of time so that the last few days can be spent in mastering the material, *and not in trying to understand the basic concepts*. Cramming at the last moment for an exam is no substitute for daily preparations and reviews. By managing time carefully and keeping up with your studies, you will have plenty of time to review *thoroughly* and clear up any questions. This will allow you to get sufficient rest before the exam and to feel confident in your preparation. Because both your physical condition and general attitude are important factors in exam performance, you will automatically do better. Proper reviewing techniques also aid retention of material as the semester progresses and better prepare you for a comprehensive final examination.

John Harley
Eastern Kentucky University

Returning Tests

One of the most difficult but rewarding things that I do is returning tests. I have always (with a rare exception) returned tests the following class period. The test is reviewed and discussed prior to beginning new material. This helps the students to learn from the tests those things that they were unsure about before the material 'gets cold'. They are then more focused on the next material instead of being concerned about the last test. This causes some long hours of grading and planning my testing schedule to give me time to evaluate. Yet the students are very positive to this approach and seem to appreciate my efforts to give them immediate feedback.

Paul Motley
Eastern Kentucky University

Response Cards

For an oral pretest, have each student fold a sheet of paper lengthwise with a big "T" on one side and a big "F" on the other. Ask true or false questions to determine prior knowledge. Students respond by holding up the appropriate side of the paper.

> Susan Edington
> Madisonville Community College

The Post-Test Questionnaire

The period after the first test of the semester I spend reviewing the testing experience with my class (one of my hard policies is always to give back a test the following period). Before going over the correct answers and providing some vital statistics about the test, I hand out this questionnaire.

This questionnaire provides a good stepping stone into discussion. If a student tells me question II. B. was too ambiguous, we discuss it right there. If the question uncovers a concept that both the texts and I failed to bring up, I address that matter (usually throwing out the question and giving the class credit). If a particular question has a problem, I make a note eliminating or clarifying it for future tests. The questionnaire, then, allows the students input, often for the next test. It lets the student know that neither the test nor the instructor is infallible, that even dyed-in-the-wool teachers can be flexible—i.e. we both learn.

The Test: A Questionnaire

1. Did the recent test cover only the assigned material?
   Yes_____   No_____
2. Did the test cover too much material?
   Yes_____   No_____
3. Was sufficient time provided to complete the test?
   Yes_____   No_____
4. Were the directions clear?
   Yes_____   No_____
5. Were individual questions clear?
   Yes_____   No_____

---

6. Was the instructor available during the test to answer questions?
   Yes_____   No_____
7. Did the test provide a variety of question types?
   Yes_____   No_____
8. Did the teacher adequately prepare the class for the test format?
   Yes_____   No_____
9. Should test scores be curved even when there are A's and B's?
   Yes_____   No_____
10. Should grammar—including spelling—be graded?
    Yes_____   No_____
11. Did the instructor cover each question during class time?
    Yes_____   No_____
12. What were the test's major strengths?
13. What were the test's major weaknesses?

Charlie Sweet
Eastern Kentucky University

A Testing Suggestion

Multiple Choice is probably not the ideal form for tests; perceptive students often read into test items ideas that were not intended by the instructor. This sometimes leads students to conclude that two answers are equally valid or that no answer is correct. To minimize this problem, pass out a blank sheet of paper along with the test and tell students that when they find an ambiguous test item, use the paper to explain the ambiguity. Any student whose explanation convinces you that the writer understands the material in question will be given credit.

If you require that each explanation begin with a statement of which choice the student marked on the answer sheet, you will find that in most cases the correct answer has been chosen and you need not read further. Tell the students that their explanation must convince you that they know the material in question; you will not be overwhelmed with essays from each student. This technique has resulted in my students having a better attitude toward my tests and fewer "complaints" after them.

Karl Kuhn
Eastern Kentucky University

The Official Cheat-Sheet

In courses where memorization of many formulas is required—or, in fact, in any course—let them bring an "Official Cheat-Sheet" to the final. They may write on it anything they desire in their own handwriting. This not only relieves their minds from the frightful experience of going blank at an inopportune time, but relieves the teacher's mind that the honest student (of whom I feel are in the majority) is not penalized. Students have indicated that they prepare more carefully than they would otherwise have done. This in itself is a valuable review because organization, concentration, and thought must go into the formation of such a sheet.

Amy King
Eastern Kentucky University

Sample Tests

Before each hour examination, a 'sample test' is given out. If this happens to be a course which has been taught previously from the current text, the old examinations do nicely. Prior to this first hour test, the students have been accustomed to concentrating on only two or three different concepts at one time. The sample test gives them the opportunity of seeing many topics together, and before they are penalized for making a wrong decision as to which method is applicable. When they are subsequently given the actual first hour test, they are then more prepared for the transition to the complete unit, and can immediately begin work. This also eliminates the inequity if some organizations have a file on such tests which is not available to certain individuals. It is well-known that each professor has certain pet questions which will be emphasized, even though he or she may not be aware of it. Upon receipt of these sample tests, students sometimes laughingly complain that they had just paid out money to a former student for these same quizzes.

Amy King
Eastern Kentucky University

Instant Course Grades

I design my courses so that I can grade each final exam in ten minutes or less and so that as soon as I know the final exam grade I can determine the course grade. I ask each student to stay for the grading of the final, and I give them their course grade before they leave the room. Usually students take varying amounts of time to complete the final, so the process goes fast.

I have had tears andcusses, but students agree that they like knowing their course grades immediately. At the end of finals week often my colleagues are carrying around boxes of papers, and I am whistling to myself. My wife and I have seven children, and our children have always been irritated at not knowing their grades for weeks after the semester is over. Grades are so important during the semester, why don't they matter at all afterwards?

George Brosi
Eastern Kentucky University

The Grade Record Sheet

Along with the syllabus I pass out a "Grade Record Sheet." It is designed to make figuring student grades simple and easy. I ask students to keep track of their own papers and to record their own grades. On the last day of class I go through their "portfolios" of papers and double-check each student's figures. Then we figure how various grades on the final will affect the course grade.

This saves me the time of recording grades and the time and space of keeping track of papers, keeps students from suspecting that I did them wrong, and keeps me from being tempted to grade a paper on the basis of what a student "deserves" as an overall average. Most important, it gets across the principle that students are responsible for their own learning. I do not think I've ever been snookered as a result. My memory is pretty good, and my handwriting is downright awful, so I'm confident that no grades have been changed on me!

George Brosi
Eastern Kentucky University

Recognizing Student Answers

Many assignments and tests have at least as many answers as students in the class. After grading the assignment or test, the instructor can go back over them, question-by-question and pick out students who gave particularly good answers. Sure, sometimes one student does a great job on just about all of them while other students have few decent answers. Still, a little juggling will allow a pleasantly even distribution of "good answers." Then the papers can be arranged in the right order to read off the good answers to each question in the order they appeared, and class can start with the instructor reading and commenting on the answers. A variation is to make notes on who did well on each question and then call on the pre-chosen student to read the answer to each particular question. In my literature classes, I require what I call a "Summary Sheet." The questions on this sheet range from the lifetime of an author—which almost everybody gets right—to the author's contribution to world literature. Somebody in the class has a good answer to each question, so even the poorest students can get a little recognition.

George Brosi
Eastern Kentucky University

Remarks Sheet

If the instructor would like to make longer comments on a paper than is feasible and/or does not have elementary-school teacher handwriting, making "remarks sheets" with letter/number codes can be extremely beneficial for the student and instructor because the instructor can say much more and give reminders for help. This particular technique has saved me hours of work and enabled my students to read more of what I write, even though I still write what I think to be too much on their papers.

For an argumentation paper, for instance, I might create a remarks sheet containing sections devoted to such areas as

- **Thesis** (T)
    T4: You are going into too much detail for the thesis. Save your explanations for support sections.
    T5: You are departing from the subject.
- **Argument** (A)

A2: You have already used this reasoning in a previous paragraph.
A8: The logic you have used is not quite sound. See *St. Martin's*, "logical fallacies," 97-98.

- **Documentation** (D)

    D12: The name and/or title you give does not match what you have in your Works Cited.
    D14: Your paraphrase is too much like the original. Review *St. Martin's*, 595-602.

Of course you might create remarks sheets to cover any number of areas. In addition to saving time on individual papers, the marks sheet can save you from writing the same comment on several papers.

Shirley Hayes
Eastern Kentucky University

IX. OUT-OF-CLASS AIDS

Some teachers seem content to limit out-of-class contact with students to chance meetings in the grill or student-initiated conferences during a few posted office hours.

Here are a few suggestions for making out-of-class contact more teacher directed and more valuable as a teaching device.

The Open Door

To try to be approachable to the students, I tell them of my "open door" policy and "book use" policy. I want students to come by my office and see me about both course work and academic progress. I want to get to know my students in an out-of-class setting. Students can borrow any book I have by filling out a 3x5 card and placing it on my desk. Since I review many books each year, I have a good professional library, and they can use it as a starting point in investigating a topic. I always try to have periods when I welcome having lunch or coffee with students. I work with my advisees in many ways other than just academic advising.

Paul Motley
Eastern Kentucky University

The End-of-Term Conference/Grade Sheet

My school has a policy whereby at mid-term I must give each student a written report assessing that student's progress in my course. I thought this report such a good idea that I've taken it a step further.

At the end of the semester, I set aside some time wherein each student must meet with me to discuss his/her final grade. During that conference I hand each student a form on which I have recorded the grade on everything the student has done for me for the semester. In addition, at the end of the form I have figured out the student's Pre-Final Average. One of the things we discuss is what grade the student must obtain on the final in order to achieve the desired course grade.

Most students love this meeting (although failing students don't like to be told so). The grade form is a convenient way to double-check each student's performance. If the student thinks I have made a mistake, I get out that student's file (in which every piece of work is kept), and we check whether that 67 was really a 76. Students also like knowing exactly what they must do on the final exam, which eliminates the "I thought I could pull a B" when they have a 52 average going in. For me, unlike in the classroom, I get to emphasize what the individual's strengths and weaknesses are. The sheet also forces me to keep up with grading, and having the Pre-Final Average figured early makes coming up with each final grade after grading the last exam much easier.

ENGLISH 101   Name_____

Grade Sheet

The information below is a compilation of what you have accomplished this semester. Double check each grade to be certain.

Paragraph I	_____
Sentence Test	_____
Paragraph II	_____
Theme I	_____
Theme II	_____
Essay Test	_____
Quiz Average	_____
Assignments	_____

TOTAL _____
Course Average _____ (Total / 8)

GRADE RANGE:
A = 90-100
B = 80- 89
C = 70- 79
D = 60- 69
F = 0- 59

Charlie Sweet
Eastern Kentucky University

Credit for Conferencing

I have taught classes which meet every other Friday. For these classes I like for the Friday format to be different. One way to achieve this is to put ten-minute time slots up on the blackboard and ask students to sign up for a time for one-on-one conferencing with the instructor on a work in progress or a paper just handed in. Students can be told that if they come for a conference earlier in the week during office hours, they will get credit for attending the Friday class without having to drive to campus that day. An alternative for classes with other formats is to count conferencing equivalent to class attendance for, say, five of the thirty class meetings. Then students can make up missed classes and attendance can be required while achieving some flexibility. When a long-lasting assignment is at a crucial phase, of course, class may be canceled in favor of obligatory conferences.

George Brosi
Eastern Kentucky University

Check-Up Notes

In addition to opening my office library for student perusal, I make available to them a notebook containing lecture notes, key terminology, and background research materials. If students miss a class or simply want to check their class notes, they can drop by and browse through this notebook.

I feared that some students might abuse this privilege, substituting a quick visit to my office for class attendance, but this has not been the case. In fact, the majority of visits are from students with excellent attendance who simply want to check-up on the material.

A bonus from this policy is getting to know students better on an individual basis and often even having an *ad hoc* seminar when several students drop by at the same time.

Anon.

X. COURSE EVALUATIONS

Teaching is an ever-changing process. Effective teachers realize that they must constantly adjust their classes in material, presentation, exercises, assignments, and testing in order to maintain student interest, involvement and learning.

But how can you know what is working and what needs to be changed? Of course, talking with students can provide some valuable information, but as the tips below suggest, strategies exist to allow you even deeper insights into the effectiveness of your class.

Glads and Wishes

I have a course wrap focus called "Glads and Wishes." A colleague (non-academic) shared it with me, and we use it for professional workshops we teach. I've found it to be very effective with both undergraduate and graduate nursing students. I simply ask each student to share things/activities/course requirements, etc. that he or she is "glad" we did in the class. I allow enough time for us to do this verbally. I usually try to start with students who are a little more assertive so shyer students have time to "warm-up." After the "glads," we process the same way with "wishes" (things we would like to have done in the class, or things they think other students would benefit from). I try to warm students up to do this by staying away from value connotations such as good and bad to reduce intimidation factors. I also participate, usually last, but I have gone first if I have a really shy group.

Pam Moore
Eastern Kentucky University

Class Assessment

Use a positive approach to the end-of-semester class evaluations. Complete a simple assessment of each class. Encourage the students to candidly list the strengths of the class and the areas for improvement. Tell them that this is their opportunity to provide input to assess the class. They are usually very honest and have some excellent suggestions. Pay attention to what they have to say!

Steve Fardo
Eastern Kentucky University

The Midterm Evaluation

So often we have our students evaluate the course at term's end and find that they have been frustrated by certain aspects of the class all semester. Since most students shy away from addressing such frustrations outwardly, they've let the situation fester for months and give it to us in that final evaluation. We in turn feel frustrated and make a mental note to address the situation next semester.

As a way to head off such dual frustration, I administer a midterm evaluation. This brief, non-threatening sheet simply asks students anonymously to let me know one thing they like about the class, one thing they dislike, and a suggestion for change. I keep the sheet brief so that the process takes only a few minutes and doesn't call on students to craft paragraphs on their feelings. I always let them know the evaluation is coming up so that they can be thinking about their responses.

Students like this evaluation since it gives them a chance to have input during the semester rather than simply commenting on things after the fact. They also gain confidence that I really care about their feelings and want to shape the class for maximum benefit.

Marsha Blythe
University of Kentucky

Advice To A Friend

Getting students to give an honest evaluation of a course is sometimes difficult. To help them say what they really feel, I have them evaluate my class in the form of a note they write to a good friend who is considering taking me the next semester.

I tell students to write in a comfortable style and familiar voice, letting their friend in on what really goes on in my class. I encourage them to use humor, sarcasm, or any other technique as long as they're honest in their estimate. I do prohibit profanity although bits have slipped into the anonymous offerings.

Students seem to "get into" these evaluations. I hardly ever get the traditional "Class was great" or "What a waste of time" responses. Rather, I get well-thought-out evaluations that get to the heart of what makes a class work.

Anon.

Write A Letter

To enable the student and teacher to communicate more openly, letter writing can be helpful. Have students write a letter at least twice during the semester in which they discuss areas of concern—e.g., if the student is having any particular problems with assignments, what the instructor is doing that is helpful or not helpful, etc. Then you can write on the student letter and return it or write a separate letter to the student.

I've found that this strategy makes students feel that they really have a voice in what goes on in class and that I care about what they think.

Shirley Hayes
Eastern Kentucky University

AFTERWORD: EFFECTIVE TEACHERS

What you have just been reading is not, for the most part, abstract theory nor is it what you might learn in a teaching methods class. The previous tips are examples and procedures that have actually worked in a college classroom.

Collectively, these tips also reveal something about good teachers. Simply put, effective teachers demonstrate a few common traits.

Effective teachers are:

- organized (they have a plan for the semester as a whole, the various units within the term, and the daily class)
- unified (classes are strung together like a necklace of fine pearls, each one beautiful, but exquisite when seen as a whole)
- cohesive (each day's class begins with goals, works toward these goals, then sums up what has been accomplished)
- experimental (they are willing to take risks, to try new things—like you in reading this book)
- energetic (they constantly work during class as well as before, encouraging the class to share their energy)
- enthusiastic (they are positive about the class)
- diverse (they vary class presentations to make the most of student learning styles)
- interactive (they employ strategies and exercises that draw students out of themselves, that prod them to learn more than they think they're capable of)
- concerned (they make an effort to get to know their students immediately, and throughout the term they nurture that relationship)
- knowledgeable (they know the material, and they constantly upgrade their knowledge through research)
- aware (they know their students, the campus environment, and current events in their students' world)

- open-minded (they are willing to accept change, newness, others' opinions)

- civil (they show respect for students and student ideas)

- in control (they steer students toward the established goals rather than driving them)

Perhaps good teachers do not consciously try to be role models. Nevertheless, they realize they cannot ask their students to be on time, prepared, alert, respectful, and energetic unless they are.